Socialism and the Irish Rebellion

Writings From James Connolly

James Connolly

Red and Black Publishers, St Petersburg, Florida

Library of Congress Cataloging-in-Publication Data

Connolly, James, 1868-1916.
  Socialism and the Irish Rebellion : writings from James Connolly / James Connolly.
     p. cm.
  ISBN 978-1-934941-36-2
1. Socialism--Ireland--History--20th century. 2. Labor movement--Ireland--History--20th century. 3. Ireland--Politics and government--1901-1910. 4. Ireland--Politics and government--1910-1921. 5. Ireland--History--Easter Rising, 1916. 6. Ireland--Social conditions--20th century. 7. Working class--Ireland--Political activity--History--20th century. I. Title.
  HX250.3.A6C665 2008
  941.5082'1--dc22

2008026347

Red and Black Publishers, PO Box 7542, St Petersburg, Florida, 33734

Contact us at: info@RedandBlackPublishers.com

Printed and manufactured in the United States of America

Contents

Socialism and Nationalism   5
Socialism and Irish Nationalism   9
State Monopoly Versus Socialism   13
Socialism and Religion: The Known and the Unknowable   17
Socialism And Political Reformers   21
Physical Force in Irish Politics   25
The Economic Basis of Politics: The Stomach, not the Brain   29
Imperialism and Socialism   33
Dogma and Food   39
Let Us Free Ireland!   43
Difficulties of Socialism   45
Home Thrusts   49
Parliamentary Democracy   53
An Object Lesson   57
Unpatriotic?   61
Declaration of Principles of the Irish Socialist Federation   65
A Political Party of the Workers   69
Sinn Féin And Socialism   73
Industrial Unionism and Constructive Socialism   81
Sinn Fein, Socialism and the Nation   87
Ballots, Bullets, Or —   91
Erin's Hope: The End & The Means   97
Industrialism and the Trade Unions   121
Sweatshops Behind the Orange Flag   131
Direct Action in Belfast   137

British Labour and Irish Politicians   141
Labour and the Proposed Partition of Ireland   149
Ireland and Ulster: An Appeal to the Working Class   151
Independent Labour Party of Ireland: Ireland Upon The Dissecting Table   155
The Problem of Trade Union Organization   159
A Continental Revolution   165
A Martyr For Conscience Sake   169
The War Upon The German Nation   173
The Friends of Small Nationalities   179
The Ballot or the Barricades   183
Rally for Labour   187
Courtsmartial and Revolution   191
Revolutionary Unionism and War   195
Insurrectionary Warfare   201
Liberty and Labour   233
What is a Scab?   237
For the Citizen Army   241
Conscription   245
Economic Conscription   249
The Call To Arms   257
The Irish Flag   261

Socialism and Nationalism

(1897)

In Ireland at the present time there are at work a variety of agencies seeking to preserve the national sentiment in the hearts of the people.

These agencies, whether Irish Language movements, Literary Societies or Commemoration Committees, are undoubtedly doing a work of lasting benefit to this country in helping to save from extinction the precious racial and national history, language and characteristics of our people.

Nevertheless, there is a danger that by too strict an adherence to their present methods of propaganda, and consequent neglect of vital living issues, they may only succeed in stereotyping our historical studies into a worship of the past, or crystallising nationalism into a tradition – glorious and heroic indeed, but still only a tradition.

Now traditions may, and frequently do, provide materials for a glorious martyrdom, but can never be strong enough to ride the storm of a successful revolution.

If the national movement of our day is not merely to re-enact the old sad tragedies of our past history, it must show itself capable of rising to the exigencies of the moment.

It must demonstrate to the people of Ireland that our nationalism is not merely a morbid idealising of the past, but is also capable of formulating a distinct and definite answer to the problems of the present and a political and economic creed capable of adjustment to the wants of the future.

This concrete political and social ideal will best be supplied, I believe, by the frank acceptance on the part of all earnest nationalists of the Republic as their goal.

Not a Republic, as in France, where a capitalist monarchy with an elective head parodies the constitutional abortions of England, and in open alliance with the Muscovite despotism brazenly flaunts its apostasy to the traditions of the Revolution.

Not a Republic as in the United States, where the power of the purse has established a new tyranny under the forms of freedom; where, one hundred years after the feet of the last British red-coat polluted the streets of Boston, British landlords and financiers impose upon American citizens a servitude compared with which the tax of pre-Revolution days was a mere trifle.

No! the Republic I would wish our fellow-countrymen to set before them as their ideal should be of such a character that the mere mention of its name would at all times serve as a beacon-light to the oppressed of every land, at all times holding forth promise of freedom and plenteousness as the reward of their efforts on its behalf.

To the tenant farmer, ground between landlordism on the one hand and American competition on the other, as between the upper and the nether millstone; to the wage-workers in the towns, suffering from the exactions of the slave-driving capitalist to the agricultural labourer, toiling away his life for a wage barely sufficient to keep body and soul together; in fact to every one of the toiling millions upon whose misery the outwardly-splendid fabric of our modern civilisation is reared, the Irish Republic might be made a word to conjure with – a rallying point for the disaffected, a haven for the oppressed, a point of departure for the Socialist, enthusiastic in the cause of human freedom.

This linking together of our national aspirations with the hopes of the men and women who have raised the standard of revolt against that system of capitalism and landlordism, of which the British Empire is the most aggressive type and resolute defender, should not, in any sense, import an element of discord into the ranks of earnest nationalists, and would serve to place us in touch with fresh reservoirs of moral and physical strength sufficient to lift the cause of Ireland to a more commanding position than it has occupied since the day of Benburb.

It may be pleaded that the ideal of a Socialist Republic, implying, as it does, a complete political and economic revolution, would be sure to alienate all our middle-class and aristocratic supporters, who would dread the loss of their property and privileges.

What does this objection mean? That we must conciliate the privileged classes in Ireland!

But you can only disarm their hostility by assuring them that in a free Ireland their 'privileges' will not be interfered with. That is to say, you must guarantee that when Ireland is free of foreign domination, the green-coated Irish soldiers will guard the fraudulent gains of capitalist and landlord from 'the thin hands of the poor' just as remorselessly and just as effectually as the scarlet-coated emissaries of England do today.

On no other basis will the classes unite with you. Do you expect the masses to fight for this ideal?

When you talk of freeing Ireland, do you only mean the chemical elements which compose the soil of Ireland? Or is it the Irish people you mean? If the latter, from what do you propose to free them? From the rule of England?

But all systems of political administration or governmental machinery are but the reflex of the economic forms which underlie them.

English rule in England is but the symbol of the fact that English conquerors in the past forced upon this country a property system founded upon spoliation, fraud and murder: that, as the present-day exercise of the 'rights of property' so originated involves the continual practice of legalised spoliation and fraud, English rule is found to be the most suitable form of government by which the spoliation can be protected, and an English army the most pliant tool with which to execute judicial murder when the fears of the propertied classes demand it.

The Socialist who would destroy, root and branch, the whole brutally materialistic system of civilisation, which like the English language we have adopted as our own, is, I hold, a far more deadly foe to English rule and tutelage, than the superficial thinker who imagines it possible to reconcile Irish freedom with those insidious but disastrous forms of economic subjection – landlord tyranny, capitalist fraud and unclean usury; baneful fruits of the Norman Conquest, the unholy trinity, of which Strongbow and Diarmuid MacMurchadha – Norman thief and Irish traitor – were the fitting precursors and apostles.

If you remove the English army to-morrow and hoist the green flag over Dublin Castle, unless you set about the organisation of the Socialist Republic your efforts would be in vain.

England would still rule you. She would rule you through her capitalists, through her landlords, through her financiers, through the whole array of commercial and individualist institutions she has planted in this country and watered with the tears of our mothers and the blood of our martyrs.

England would still rule you to your ruin, even while your lips offered hypocritical homage at the shrine of that Freedom whose cause you had betrayed.

Nationalism without Socialism – without a reorganisation of society on the basis of a broader and more developed form of that common property which underlay the social structure of Ancient Erin — is only national recreancy.

It would be tantamount to a public declaration that our oppressors had so far succeeded in inoculating us with their perverted conceptions of justice and morality that we had finally decided to accept those conceptions as our own, and no longer needed an alien army to force them upon us.

As a Socialist I am prepared to do all one man can do to achieve for our motherland her rightful heritage – independence; but if you ask me to abate one jot or tittle of the claims of social justice, in order to conciliate the privileged classes, then I must decline.

Such action would be neither honourable nor feasible. Let us never forget that he never reaches Heaven who marches thither in the company of the Devil. Let us openly proclaim our faith: the logic of events is with us.

Socialism and Irish Nationalism

(1897)

The public life of Ireland has been generally so much identified with the struggle for political emancipation, that, naturally, the economic side of the situation has only received from our historians and public men a very small amount of attention.

Scientific Socialism is based upon the truth incorporated in this proposition of Karl Marx, that, "the economic dependence of the workers on the monopolists of the means of production is the foundation of slavery in all its forms, the cause of nearly all social misery, modern crime, mental degradation and political dependence". Thus this false exaggeration of purely political forms which has clothed in Ireland the struggle for liberty, must appear to the Socialist an inexplicable error on the part of a people so strongly crushed down as the Irish.

But the error is more in appearance than in reality.

The reactionary attitude of our political leaders notwithstanding, the great mass of the Irish people know full well that if they had once conquered that political liberty which they struggle for with so much ardour, it would have to be used as a means of social redemption before their well-being would be assured.

In spite of occasional exaggeration of its immediate results one must remember that by striving determinedly, as they have done, towards this definite political end, the Irish are working on the lines of conduct laid down by modern Socialism as the indispensable condition of success.

Since the abandonment of the unfortunate insurrectionism of the early Socialists whose hopes were exclusively concentrated on the eventual triumph of an uprising and barricade struggle, modern Socialism, relying on the slower, but surer method of the ballot-box, has directed the attention of its partisans toward the peaceful conquest of the forces of government in the interests of the revolutionary ideal.

The advent of Socialism can only take place when the revolutionary proletariat, in possession of the organized forces of the nation (the political power of government) will be able to build up a social organization in conformity with the natural march of industrial development.

On the other hand, non-political co-operative effort must infallibly succumb in face of the opposition of the privileged classes, entrenched behind the ramparts of law and monopoly. This is why, even when he is from the economic point of view intensely conservative, the Irish Nationalist, even with his false reasoning, is an active agent in social regeneration, in so far as he seeks to invest with full power over its own destinies a people actually governed in the interests of a feudal aristocracy.

The section of the Socialist army to which I belong, the Irish Socialist Republican Party, never seeks to hide its hostility to those purely bourgeois parties which at present direct Irish politics.

But, in inscribing on our banners an ideal to which they also give lip-homage, we have no intention of joining in a movement which could debase the banner of revolutionary Socialism.

The Socialist parties of France oppose the mere Republicans without ceasing to love the Republic. In the same way the Irish Socialist Republican Party seeks the independence of the nation, while refusing to conform to the methods or to employ the arguments of the chauvinist Nationalist.

As Socialists we are not imbued with national or racial hatred by the remembrance that the political and social order under which we live was imposed on our fathers at the point of the sword; that during 700 years Ireland has resisted this unjust foreign domination; that famine, pestilence and bad government have made this western isle almost a desert and scattered our exiled fellow-countrymen over the whole face of the globe.

The enunciation of facts such as I have just stated is not able today to inspire or to direct the political energies of the militant working class of Ireland; such is not the foundation of our resolve to free Ireland from the yoke of the British Empire. We recognize rather that during all these centuries the great mass of the British people had no political existence whatever; that England was, politically and socially, terrorized by a numerically small governing class; that the atrocities which have been perpetrated against Ireland are only imputable to the unscrupulous ambition of this class, greedy to enrich itself at the expense of defenceless men; that up to the present generation the great majority of the English people were denied a deliberate voice in the government of their own country; that it is, therefore, manifestly unjust to charge the English people with the past crimes of their Government; and that at the worst we can but charge them with a criminal apathy in submitting to slavery and allowing themselves to be made an instrument of coercion for the enslavement of others. An accusation as applicable to the present as to the past.

But whilst refusing to base our political action on hereditary national antipathy, and wishing rather comradeship with the English workers than to regard them with hatred, we desire with our precursors the United Irishmen of 1798 that our animosities be buried with the bones of our ancestors – there is not a party in Ireland which accentuates more as a vital principle of its political faith the need of separating Ireland from England and of making it absolutely independent. In the eyes of the ignorant and of the unreflecting this appears an inconsistency, but I am persuaded that our Socialist brothers in France will immediately recognize the justice of the reasoning upon which such a policy is based.

1. We hold "the economic emancipation of the worker requires the conversion of the means of production into the common property of Society". Translated into the current language and practice of actual politics this teaches that the necessary road to be travelled towards the establishment of Socialism requires the transference of the means

of production from the hands of private owners to those of public bodies directly responsible to the entire community.

2. Socialism seeks then in the interest of the democracy to strengthen popular action on all public bodies.

3. Representative bodies in Ireland would express more directly the will of the Irish people than when those bodies reside in England.

An Irish Republic would then be the natural depository of popular power; the weapon of popular emancipation, the only power which would show in the full light of day all these class antagonisms and lines of economic demarcation now obscured by the mists of bourgeois patriotism.

In that there is not a trace of chauvinism. We desire to preserve with the English people the same political relations as with the people of France, or Germany, or of any other country; the greatest possible friendship, but also the strictest independence. Brothers, but not bedfellows. Thus, inspired by another ideal, conducted by reason not by tradition, following a different course, the Socialist Republican Party of Ireland arrives at the same conclusion as the most irreconcilable Nationalist. The governmental power of England over us must be destroyed; the bonds which bind us to her must be broken. Having learned from history that all bourgeois movements end in compromise, that the bourgeois revolutionists of today become the conservatives of tomorrow, the Irish Socialists refuse to deny or to lose their identity with those who only half understand the problem of liberty. They seek only the alliance and the friendship of those hearts who, loving liberty for its own sake, are not afraid to follow its banner when it is uplifted by the hands of the working class who have most need of it. Their friends are those who would not hesitate to follow that standard of liberty, to consecrate their lives in its service even should it lead to the terrible arbitration of the sword.

State Monopoly Versus Socialism

(June 1899)

One of the most significant signs of our times is the readiness with which our struggling middle class turns to schemes of State or Municipal ownership and control, for relief from the economic pressure under which it is struggling. Thus we find in England demands for the nationalisation of the telephone system, for the extension of municipal enterprise in the use of electricity, for the extension of the parcel system in the Post Office, for the nationalisation of railways and canals. In Ireland we have our middle class reformers demanding state help for agriculture, state purchase of lands, arterial draining, state construction of docks, piers and harbours, state aid for the fishing industry, state control of the relations between agricultural tenant and landlord, and also nationalisation of railways and canals. There is a certain section of Socialists, chiefly in England, who never tire of hailing all such demands for state activity as a sign of the growth of the Socialist spirit among the middle class, and therefore worthy of all the support the working-class democracy can give. In some degree such a view seems justifiable. The fact that large sections of the capitalist class join in demanding the intervention of the State in industry is a sure sign that they, at least, have lost the overweening belief in the all-sufficiency of private enterprise which characterised their class a generation ago; and that they have been forced to recognise the fact that there are a multitude of things in which the 'brain', 'self-reliance', and 'personal responsibility' of the capitalist are entirely unnecessary. To argue that, since in such enterprises the private property-holder is dispensed with, therefore he can be dispensed with in all other forms of industrial activity, is logical enough and we really fail to see in what manner the advocates of capitalist society can continue to clamour for such state ownership as that alluded to – ownership in which the private capitalist is seen to be superfluous, and yet continue to argue that in all other forms of industry the private capitalist is indispensable. For it must be remembered that every function of a useful character performed by the State or Municipality to-day was at one time performed by private individuals for profit, and in conformity with the then generally accepted belief that it could not be satisfactorily performed except by private individuals.

But all this notwithstanding, we would, without undue desire to carp or cavil, point out that to call such demands 'Socialistic' is in the highest degree misleading. Socialism properly implies above all things the co-operative control by the workers of the machinery of production; without this co-operative control the public ownership by the State is not Socialism – it is only State capitalism. The demands of the middle-class reformers, from the Railway Reform League down, are simply plans to facilitate the business transactions of the capitalist class. State Telephones – to cheapen messages in the interest of the middle class who are the principal users of the telephone system; State Railways – to cheapen carriage of goods in the interest of the middle-class trader; State-construction of piers, docks, etc. – in the interest of the middle-class merchant; in fact every scheme now advanced in which the help of the State is invoked is a scheme to lighten the burden of the capitalist – trader, manufacturer, or farmer. Were they all in working order to-morrow the change would not necessarily benefit the working class; we would still have in our state industries, as in the Post Office to-day, the same unfair classification of salaries, and the same despotic rule of an irresponsible head. Those who worked most and hardest would still get the least remuneration, and the rank and file would still be deprived of all voice in the ordering of their industry, just the same as in all private enterprises.

Therefore, we repeat, state ownership and control is not necessarily Socialism – if it were, then the Army, the Navy, the Police, the Judges, the Gaolers, the Informers, and the Hangmen, all would all be Socialist functionaries, as they are State officials – but the ownership by the State of all the land and materials for labour, combined with the co-operative control by the workers of such land and materials, would be Socialism.

Schemes of state and municipal ownership, if unaccompanied by this co-operative principle, are but schemes for the perfectioning of the mechanism of capitalist government—schemes to make the capitalist regime respectable and efficient for the purposes of the capitalist; in the second place they represent the class-conscious instinct of the business man who feels that capitalist should not prey upon capitalist, while all may unite to prey upon the workers. The chief immediate sufferers from private ownership of railways, canals, and telephones are the middle class shop-keeping element, and their resentment at the tariffs imposed is but the capitalist political expression of the old adage that "dog should not eat dog."

It will thus be seen that an immense gulf separates the 'nationalising' proposals of the middle class from the 'socialising' demands of the revolutionary working class. The first proposes to endow a Class State – repository of the political power of the Capitalist Class – with certain powers and functions to be administered in the common interest of the possessing class; the second proposes to subvert the Class State and replace it with the Socialist State, representing organised society – the Socialist Republic. To the cry of the middle class reformers, "make this or that the property of the government," we reply, "yes, in proportion as the workers are ready to make the government their property."

Socialism and Religion: The Known and the Unknowable

(June 1899)

Perhaps upon no point are the doctrines of Socialism so much misunderstood, and so much misrepresented, as in their relation to Religion. When driven into a corner upon every other point at issue; when from the point of view of economics, of politics, or of morality, he is worsted in argument, this question of Religion invariably forms the final entrenchment of the enemy of Socialism – especially in Ireland.

"But it is opposed to Religion," constitutes the last words, the ultimate shift of the supporters of capitalism, driven from every other line of defence but stubbornly refusing to yield. "Socialism is Atheism, and all Socialists are Atheists," or "Your Socialism is but a fine name to cover your Atheism in its attack upon the Church;" all these phrases are so commonly heard in the course of every dispute upon the merits or demerits of the Socialist doctrine that we require no apology for introducing them here in order to point their illogical character. So far from it being true that Socialism and Atheism are synonymous terms, it is a curious and instructive fact that almost all the prominent propagandists of Freethought in our generation have been, and are, most determined enemies of Socialism. The late Charles

Bradlaugh, in his time the most aggressive Freethinker in England, was to the last resolute and uncompromising in his hatred of Socialism; G.W. Foote, the present editor of the *Freethinker*, the national organ of English Secularism, is a bitter enemy of Socialism, and the late Colonel Bob Ingersoll, the chief apostle of Freethought doctrine in the United States, was well known as an apologist of capitalism.

On the continent of Europe many other quite similar cases might he recorded, but those already quoted will suffice, as being those most easily verified by our readers. It is a suggestive and amusing fact that in the motley ranks of the defenders of Capitalism the professional propagandists of Freethought are comrades-in-arms of His Holiness the Pope; the ill-reasoned and inconclusive Encyclicals lately issued against Socialism make of the hierarchy of the Catholic Church belated camp followers in the armies marching under the banners raised by the agnostic exponents of the individualist philosophy. Obviously, even the meanest intelligence can see that there need be no identity of thought between the Freethinker as such, and the Socialist as a Socialist. From what then does the popular misconception arise? In the first instance from the interested attempt of the propertied classes to create such a prejudice against Socialism as might deter the working class giving ear to its doctrines – an attempt too often successful; and in the second instance, from a misconception of the attitude of the Socialist party towards the theological dogma in general. The Socialist Party of Ireland prohibits the discussion of theological or anti-theological questions at its meetings, public or private. This is in conformity with the practice of the chief Socialist parties of the world, which have frequently, in Germany for example, declared Religion to be a private matter, and outside the scope of Socialist action. Modern Socialism, in fact, as it exists in the minds of its leading exponents, and as it is held and worked for by an increasing number of enthusiastic adherents throughout the civilised world, has an essentially material, matter-of-fact foundation. We do not mean that its supporters are necessarily materialists in the vulgar, and merely anti-theological, sense of the term, but that they do not base their Socialism upon any interpretation of the language or meaning of Scripture, nor upon the real or supposed intentions of a beneficent Deity. They as a party neither affirm or deny those things, but leave it to the individual conscience of each member to determine what beliefs on such questions they shall hold. As a political party they wisely prefer to take their stand upon the actual phenomena of social life as they can be observed in operation amongst us to-day, or as they can be traced in the recorded facts of history. If any special interpretation of the meanings of Scripture tends to influence human thought in the direction of Socialism, or is found to be on a plane with the postulates of Socialist doctrine, then the scientific Socialist considers that the said interpretation is stronger because of its identity with the teachings of Socialism, but he does not necessarily believe that Socialism is stronger, or its position more impregnable, because of its theological ally. He realises that the facts upon which his Socialist faith are based are strong enough in themselves to withstand every shock, and attacks from every quarter, and therefore while he is at all times willing to accept help from every extraneous source, he will only accept it on one condition, viz., that he is not to be required in return to identify his cause with any other whose discomfiture might also involve Socialism in discredit. This is the main reason why Socialists fight shy of theological dogmas and religions generally: because we feel that Socialism is based upon a series of facts requiring only unassisted human reason to grasp and master all their details, whereas Religion of every kind is admittedly based upon 'faith' in the occurrence in past ages of a series of phenomena inexplicable by any process of mere human reasoning. Obviously, therefore, to identify Socialism with Religion would be to abandon at once that universal, non-sectarian character which to-day we find indispensable to working-class unity, as it would mean that our members would be required to conform to one religious creed, as well as to one specific economic faith – a course of action we have no intention of entering upon as it would inevitably entangle us in the disputes of the warring sects of the world, and thus lead to the disintegration of the Socialist Party.

Socialism, as a party, bases itself upon its knowledge of facts, of economic truths, and leaves the building up of religious ideals or faiths to the outside public, or to its individual members if they so will. It is neither Freethinker nor Christian, Turk nor Jew, Buddhist nor Idolator, Mahommedan nor Parsee – it is only human.

Socialism And Political Reformers

(July 1899)

Among the many developments of Socialist activity at which the man in the street is apt to be astonished, perhaps none are more difficult to comprehend at first sight than the implacable hostility shown by the Socialist parties of the world towards the political parties hitherto identified with the agitation for political reform. The uninitiated find it hard to understand why there should be such marked hostility between parties, both of whom place on their programme planks of political reform seemingly almost identical in character; why the Socialist party, which represents the most revolutionary ideas of our day, should seek the downfall of political reform parties with a zest and eagerness which the most bigoted Conservative could never hope to excel. It is observed that wherever the Socialist party is strong, as in Germany, France, or Belgium, it is the Liberal party – the party of mere political reformers – which has been the first to suffer in loss of prestige and membership in exact proportion as Socialism has advanced.

Strange though the circumstance may seem to the unreflective mind, it is but what might have been expected to result from the appearance upon the political field of a force which, like the Socialist party, had at once a programme of political reform embracing all and more than the old reform parties had striven for, and a programme embodying demands for economic changes which receive no support from middle-class reformers, though a crying necessity of the times. The development of acute economic problems, side by side with the extension of the franchise – economic problems are, in fact, most acute in the politically freest countries – has borne in upon the minds of the working-class voters the conviction that, except as a means to an end, political freedom is a valueless acquisition for their class. They therefore demand the right to use that political power in the direction of their own class interests, but on making such demand are surprised to see their quondam middle-class leaders the first to denounce them and call upon the State to oppose them. When this point has been reached, as in the countries above named and to a lesser degree in England and America, the thoughtful observer of politics cannot but see that middle-class parties of reform have outlived their usefulness; that whatever political change is still required to establish the democracy in power can be sought for as well under the banner of the new political force of Socialism as under the old banner of Liberalism, and that this new power by basing its agitation upon the material wants of the producing class gathers to its aid a potential power, in the passion and self-interest of the majority of the nation, which the mere doctrinaires – Liberal, Radical, or Republican – could never hope to rally. Therefore political reform parties decay as the Socialist Parties thrive; the latter early the political demands of the former on their banner side by side with the economic demands of their class, and thus deprived of their sole reason for existence the capitalist reform parties lose their attraction for the multitude – now pressing eagerly onward to the inspiration of a new and better hope.

On the other hand Conservatism is, as a party, secure of an existence as long as the present system lasts. It may be set down as an axiom that there will always be a Conservative party as long as there is tyranny and privilege to conserve. Hence we find the old reform parties shedding their members at both ends – the wealthier section falling over into the ranks of Conservatism, in order to strengthen the only party able to defend their monopolies, and the working class section joining hands with the Socialists as the only party embracing the cause alike of political and industrial liberty. The Socialists are naturally desirous of hastening this process, in order that the political battlefield may be left clear and open for the final struggle between the only two parties possessed of a logical reason for existence – the Conservative party defending the strongholds of monarchy, aristocracy and capitalism; and the Socialist party storming those strongholds in the interest of human freedom. This consummation cannot be realised as long as there exists a political party which, like the Liberals of England and the Continent, and the Home Rule parties of Ireland, attempts to blend the principles of progress and reaction – now blatantly declaring for political freedom, now vigorously defending economic slavery. Therefore the Socialists uniformly seek the discomfiture of Liberalism, regarding it as a buffer between the contending forces of tyranny and freedom; and hence the clear-sighted workmen of the Continent have already reduced that once formidable party to a mere cypher in politics, and will before long completely wipe it out of existence.

The fact is not without its lesson to us here in Ireland. We too have so-called parties of reform – Home Rule in all its phases is now but a cloak for the designs of the middle class desirous of making terms with the Imperial Government it pretends to dislike. It is but capitalist Liberalism, speaking with an Irish accent. As such it is the enemy of every effort at working-class emancipation, and if the workers of Ireland as are alive to the interests of their class as are their brethren on the Continent, they will help build up that Socialist Party which is destined to march over the grave of Home Rule Liberalism to the final assault and destruction of the strongholds of oppression.

Physical Force in Irish Politics

(July 1899)

Ireland occupies a position among the nations of the earth unique in a great variety of its aspects, but in no one particular is this singularity more marked than in the possession of what is known as a 'physical force party' – a party, that is to say, whose members are united upon no one point, and agree upon no single principle, except upon the use of physical force as the sole means of settling the dispute between the people of this country and the governing power of Great Britain.

Other countries and other peoples have, from time to time, appealed to what the first French Revolutionists picturesquely described as the "sacred right of insurrection," but in so appealing they acted under the inspiration of, and combated for, some great governing principle of political or social life upon which they, to a man, were in absolute agreement. The latter-day high falutin 'hillside' man, on the other hand, exalts into a principle that which the revolutionists of other countries have looked upon as a weapon, and in his gatherings prohibits all discussion of those principles which formed the main strength of his prototypes elsewhere and made the successful use of that weapon possible. Our people have glided at different periods of the past century from moral force agitation, so-called, into physical force rebellion, from constitutionalism into insurrectionism, meeting in each the same failure and the same disaster and yet seem as far as ever from learning the great truth that neither method is ever likely to be successful until they first insist that a perfect agreement upon the end to be attained should be arrived at as a starting-point of all our efforts.

To the reader unfamiliar with Irish political history such a remark seems to savour almost of foolishness, its truth is so apparent; but to the reader acquainted with the inner workings of the political movements of this country the remark is pregnant with the deepest meaning. Every revolutionary effort in Ireland has drawn the bulk of its adherents from the ranks of the disappointed followers of defeated constitutional movements. After having exhausted their constitutional efforts in striving to secure such a modicum of political power as would justify them to their own consciences in taking a place as loyal subjects of the British Empire, they, in despair, turned to thoughts of physical force as a means of attaining their ends. Their conception of what constitutes freedom was in no sense changed or revolutionised; they still believed in the political form of freedom which had been their ideal in their constitutional days; but no longer hoping for it from the acts of the British Parliament, they swung over into the ranks of the 'physical force' men as the only means of attaining it.

The so-called physical force movement of today in like manner bases its hopes upon the disgust of the people over the failure of the Home Rule movement; it seeks to enlist the people under its banners, not so much by pointing out the base ideals of the constitutionalists or the total inadequacy of their pet measures to remedy the evils under which the people suffer, as by emphasising the greater efficacy of physical force as a national weapon. Thus, the one test of an advanced Nationalist is, in their opinion, one who believes in physical force. It may be the persons so professing to believe are Republicans; it may be they are believers in monarchy; it may be that Home Rule would satisfy them; it may be that they despise Home Rule. No matter what their political faith may be, if only they are prepared to express belief in the saving grace of physical force, they are acclaimed as advanced Nationalists - worthy descendants of 'the men of '98.' The '98 Executive, organised in the commencement by professed believers in the physical force doctrine, started by proclaiming its adherence to the principle of national independence "as understood by Wolfe Tone and the United Irishmen," and in less than twelve months from doing so, deliberately rejected a similar resolution and elected on its governing body men notorious for their Royalist proclivities. As the '98 Executive represents the advanced Nationalists of Ireland, this repudiation of the Republican faith of the United Irishmen is an interesting corroboration of the truth of our statement that the advanced Nationalists of our day are utterly regardless of principle and only attach importance to methods – an instance of putting the cart before the horse, absolutely unique in its imbecility and unparalleled in the history of the world.

It may be interesting, then, to place before our readers the Socialist Republican conception of the functions and uses of physical force in a popular movement. We neither exalt it into a principle nor repudiate it as something not to be thought of. Our position towards it is that the use or non-use of force for the realisation of the ideas of progress always has been and always will be determined by the attitude, not of the party of progress, but of the governing class opposed to that party. If the time should arrive when the party of progress finds its way to freedom barred by the stubborn greed of a possessing class entrenched behind the barriers of law and order; if the party of progress has indoctrinated the people at large with the new revolutionary conception of society and is therefore representative of the will of a majority of the nation, if it has exhausted all the peaceful means at its disposal for the purpose of demonstrating to the people and their enemies that the new revolutionary ideas do possess the suffrage of the majority; then, but not till then, the party which represents the revolutionary idea is justified in taking steps to assume the powers of government, and in using the weapons of force to dislodge the usurping class or government in possession, and treating its members and supporters as usurpers and rebels against the constituted authorities always have been created. In other words, Socialists believe that the question of force is of very minor importance; the really important question is of the principles upon which is based the movement that may or may not need the use of force to realise its object.

Here, then, is the immense difference between the Socialist Republicans and our friends the physical force men. The latter, by stifling all discussions of principles, earn the passive and fleeting commendation of the unthinking multitude; the former, by insisting upon a thorough understanding of their basic principles, do not so readily attract the multitude, but do attract and hold the more thoughtful amongst them. It is the difference betwixt a mob in revolt and an army in preparation. The mob who cheer a speaker referring to the hopes of a physical force movement would, in the very hour of apparent success, be utterly disorganised and divided by the passage through the British Legislature of any trumpery Home Rule Bill. The army of class-conscious workers organising under the banner of the Socialist Republican Party, strong in their knowledge of economic truth and firmly grounded in their revolutionary principles, would remain entirely unaffected by any such manoeuvre and, knowing it would not change their position as a subject class, would still press forward, resolute and undivided, with their faces set towards their only hope of emancipation – the complete control by the working-class democracy of all the powers of National Government.

Thus the policy of the Socialist Republicans is seen to be the only wise one. "Educate that you may be free"; principles first, methods afterwards. If the advocacy of physical force failed to achieve success or even to effect an uprising when the majority were unenfranchised and the secret ballot unknown, how can it be expected to succeed now that the majority are in possession of voting power and the secret ballot safeguards the voter?

The ballot-box was given us by our masters for their purpose; let us use it for our own. Let us demonstrate at that ballot-box the strength and intelligence of the revolutionary idea; let us make the hustings a rostrum from which to promulgate our principles; let us grasp the public powers in the interest of the disinherited class; let us emulate our fathers and, like the 'true men of '98,' place ourselves in line with the most advanced thought of our age and drawing inspiration and hope from the spectacle presented by the world-wide revolt of the workers, prepare for the coming of the day when the Socialist working-class of Ireland will, through its elected representatives, present its demand for freedom from the yoke of a governing master class or nation – the day on which the question of moral or physical force shall be finally decided.

The Economic Basis of Politics: The Stomach, not the Brain

(August 1899)

Nothing more strikingly illustrates the crude and unscientific theories of the ordinary middle class politician than the desperate attempts at present being made to build up a great political party in Ireland on the lines of the late Home Rule movement. Apparently all sections of the Home Rule party are possessed with the belief that great political movements can be constructed at will, and that an effective, aggressive political force may have its origin, not deep down in the daily life of the people, but in the brains of some half dozen gentlemen in parliament. Viewed from this standpoint the toiling multitudes are mere automata, and the really effective national force is to be found in the men whom the Home Rule press and orators point out to the multitude as leaders. The truth that the political movements of a country spring from the pulsations of its economic life; that all political parties are the instruments of a class, and are great and powerful only in the proportion in which the development of the struggle for existence forces their particular class interest upon the majority of the nation as a dominant factor in their daily life – all this seems to a quite unheard of philosophy amongst capitalist politicians.

Yet a slight survey of the history of the world in general, or of Ireland in particular, could not fail to bring the truth of this eminently Socialist doctrine home to the mind of the thoughtful student of events. The great political organisations which have successfully revolutionised the systems of governments under which they lived, have had their origin, not in the brains of mighty leaders, but in the daily and hourly needs of the multitude, and have acquired force and power only in so far as those needs became sharp and pressing enough to goad that sluggard multitude to action. When at such a crisis there arose a man lucky enough, or astute enough, to make himself the mouthpiece of the discontented multitude; to coin its inarticulate groanings into political phraseology, and give its hunger-inspired desire for change in intelligent formulation, then such a man became a 'great leader', and the organisation following the course he advocated the leading political force. To the minds of the superficial middle class thinkers – always ready to believe that the world turned around their heroes and successful persons as upon its axis – the leaders had created the movement which they led; to the mind of the scientific Socialist the leaders and the movements were both the product of the quickening of intellect caused by social conditions adversely affecting the life of the people at large.

Examine the great revolutionary movements of history and you find that in all cases they sprang from unsatisfactory social conditions, and had their origin in a desire for material well being. In other words, the seat of progress and source of revolution is not in the brain, but in the stomach. The fact that this truth has hitherto been obscured, or even denied; that the pioneers of progress uniformly clothed their political demands in the most idealistic language and the most flowery phraseology; or that they constantly appealed for the support of 'all unselfish and generous souls', rather than to commonplace interests, only proves that we are all too prone to hide even from ourselves the real nature of our impelling desires, and, even when most stubbornly following our grossest instincts, to throw around our actions all the glamour of 'spiritual cravings', or 'patriotic hopes'.

The power and unconquerable optimism of the socialist party is due to their recognition of this materialist basis of history, this economic basis of polities. Knowing that their ultimate ideal and immediate demands are in a line with the progress of the human race towards prosperity, and that every scheme for better social conditions at all likely to effect its purpose must be of the nature of a step in their direction, Socialists cannot lose courage, because even in the midst of temporary defeat they know that the needs of the workers, who are in the majority, will eventually impel them into line with the Social-Revolutionary forces. From this fact our Irish politicians – and revolutionists – may gain, not comfort, perhaps, but wisdom. The history of the American Revolution, the French Revolution, the Irish Volunteers, the risings of 1798, 1848, and the Irish Land League, all bear out our argument upon the economic basis of great political movements.

The American Revolution was a revolt against the action of England in throttling the infant industries of America, and came to a head with a tax upon tea – all 'base' material reasons; the French Revolution was the revolt of an oppressed and famished people against outworn, medieval landlordism (feudalism) and the vexatious taxes upon industry imposed by a corrupt Court; the Irish Volunteer movement was, in its anti-English aspect, a revolt of the Irish manufacturing class against the restrictions put upon their trade by England, – "Free Trade, or else" was the motto they hung up on their cannon, and when that one point was gained all the 'patriotic enthusiasm' of the leaders vanished; Grattan termed the Volunteers, upon whose backs he had climbed to political eminence, 'an armed rabble', and the whole movement collapsed as suddenly as it had arisen – the economic basis being gone the patriotism was no longer evident. 1798 was an abortive Irish edition of the French Revolution – despite the lying twaddle of the present day about the society of United Irishmen being a 'Union of All Classes', there is not in history any record of a movement, except the Paris Commune, in which the classes and the masses were so sharply divided; 1848 found its inspiration in the promptings of famine – and its failure in the total incapacity of the doctrinaire Young Irelanders to understand the difference between revolutionary action and 'heroic' posings; the Land League found its inspiration in a partial failure of the crops, and in the newly developed competition of America – and the collapse of the Land League came with reduced rents and partial prosperity.

In every case the social condition of the mass of the people was the determining factor in political activity. Where the mass of the people find existing conditions intolerable, and imagine they see a way out, there will be a great political movement; where the social conditions are not so abnormally acute no amount of political oratory, nor yet co-operation of leaders, can produce a movement.

The great Labour uprising at the Irish Local Government elections of 1898 sprang up spontaneously without a leader, and despite the political parties; when the men who supported it have realised the futility of trying to effect any great improvement in their condition by the action of local bodies, they will seek for a political party which can express their class interests upon national basis – and seeking it find the Socialist Party, ready and equipped for the task. By our action to-day we are preparing the ground for more aggressive revolutionary action when the working class of Ireland at last recognise in our principles the embodiment of their hopes; firmly grounded upon our knowledge of the economic basis of all political action, we confidently await the day when the ever-increasing pressure of capitalist society shall bring the workers into our ranks and the destinies of the nation into our hands.

Imperialism and Socialism

(November 1899)

As Socialists – and therefore anxious to at all times throw the full weight of whatever influence we possess upon the side of the forces making most directly for Socialism – we have often been somewhat disturbed in our mind by observing in the writings and speeches of some of our foreign comrades a tendency to discriminate in favour of Great Britain in all the international complications in which that country may be involved over questions of territorial annexation, spheres of influence, etc., in barbarous or semi-civilised portions of the globe. We are, we repeat, disturbed in our mind upon the subject because we ourselves do not at all sympathise with this pro-British policy, but, on the contrary, would welcome the humiliation of the British arms in any one of the conflicts in which it is at present engaged, or with which it has been lately menaced. This we freely avow, but the question then arises: Is this hostility to the British Empire due to the fact of our national and racial subjection by that power, and does it exist in spite of our Socialism, or is it consistent with the doctrines we hold as adherents of the Marxist propaganda, and believers in the Marxist economics.

This is the question we propose briefly to discuss in our article this week. We are led to the discussion of this topic by observing that the English Socialists are apparently divided over the question of the war on the Transvaal; one section of the Social Democratic Federation going strongly for the Boers and against the war; another also declaring against the war, but equally denouncing the Boers; and, finally, one Socialist leader, Mr. Blatchford, editor of the *Clarion* and author of *Merrie England*, coming out bluntly for the war and toasting the health of the queen, and the "Success of the British arms". On the other hand all the journals of the party on the continent of Europe and in America, as far as we are aware, come out in this instance wholeheartedly on the side of the Transvaal and against what the organ of our Austrian comrades fittingly terms England's act of "blood-thirsty piracy".

We ask then is there no common ground upon which Socialists can agree to treat all matters of international politics – a common standpoint from which all questions of race or nationality shall be carefully excluded, and every question dealt with from the position of its effect upon the industrial development required to bring the Socialist movement to a head? Nominally all Socialists hold to the international solidarity of Labour, and the identity of the interests of the workers the world over, and during the Franco-German and Spanish-American wars the Socialists of those countries demonstrated that the belief was no mere abstract theory, but a living, concrete fact. But our English friend, Mr. Blatchford, deliberately throws the doctrine to the winds, and declares that "when England is at war he is English and regards all those who have taken up arms against England as enemies to be fought and beaten." This is unqualifiedly chauvinist, and as a brutal endorsement of every act of brigandage and murder in which the capitalists of England may involve their country it throws a curious sidelight on the mental make-up of this man – who very nearly shed tears of pity over the wrongs and "Christ-like appearance" of the Anarchists expelled from the International Socialist Congress in London. Our esteemed comrade, H.M. Hyndman of the Social Democratic Federation, also in an article contributed to the Berlin *Vorwaerts* and reprinted in *Justice* took the position that England ought not to have given way to Russia at Port Arthur, but ought to have fought her and asserted English supremacy in the far East. His reason for so contending being the greater freedom enjoyed under British than under Russian rule.

Mr. Blatchford's chauvinist pronouncement can be ignored as simply a personal predilection, and therefore binding no one, but the opinions of our comrades in the Social Democratic Federation of England hardly stand upon the same footing, but require severer consideration.

That we may not be accused of criticising the attitude of others without stating our own, we hereby place on record our position on all questions of international policy.

Scientific revolutionary Socialism teaches us that Socialism can only be realised when Capitalism has reached its zenith of development; that consequently the advance of nations industrially undeveloped into the capitalistic stage of industry is a thing highly to be desired, since such advance will breed a revolutionary proletariat in such countries and force forward here the political freedom necessary for the speedy success of the Socialist movement; and finally, that as colonial expansion and the conquest of new markets are necessary for the prolongation of the life of capitalism, the prevention of colonial expansion and the loss of markets to countries capitalistically developed, such as England, precipitates economic crises there, and so gives an impulse to revolutionary thought and helps to shorten the period required to develop backward countries and thus prepare the economic conditions needed for our triumph.

That is our position. Arguing from such premises we hold that as England is the most capitalistically developed country in Europe, every fresh conquest of territory by her armies, every sphere of influence acquired in the interests of her commercialists, is a span added to the life of capitalist society; and that every market lost, every sphere of influence captured by the non-capitalist enemies of England, shortens the life of Capitalism by aiding the development of reactionary countries, and hurling back upon itself the socially conservative industrial population of England.

Comrade Hyndman claims that we should oppose Russia because her people are ruled despotically, and favour England because her people are politically free. But that is the reasoning of a political Radical, not the dispassionate analysis of contemporary history we have a right to expect from an economist and a Socialist of Hyndman's reputation. Our comrade quite forgets to apply that materialist philosophy of history which he himself has done so much to popularise in its Marxian form, viz., that the economic system of any given society is the basis of all else in that society – its political superstructure included. If he did so apply it, he would realise that the political freedom of England is born of her capitalism. Her capitalist class required a wage slave class possessing such freedom or mobility of movement as would make them available at short notice wherever the exigencies of capitalism demanded. To gain such absolute freedom of migration a political movement had to be inaugurated placing the capitalist class in a position to break the bonds of serfdom for the labourer. This once achieved, the capitalistic concentration of the workers in great centres of population gave to the proletariat the sense of numbers and opportunities of organisation required to complete the work of political enfranchisement. Thus the economic necessities of capitalism always and everywhere beget a measure of political freedom for its slaves.

Russia is not yet a capitalist country, therefore her people bow beneath the yoke of an autocrat. This is only saying that her capitalist class is not strong enough yet to force upon the government laws establishing the conditions most helpful to capitalist development. But every forward move of Russia in the direction of colonial expansion strengthens that capitalist class in Russia and in so doing breeds there the revolutionary working class. On the other hand, if the wishes of comrade Hyndman were to be realized, Russian capitalism would be checked in its growth, and the discontent in that country, lacking capitalistic conditions, would resolve itself into a purely agrarian movement. The revolutionary proletariat would remain unborn.

Drive the Russian out of Poland! By all means! Prevent his extension towards Europe! Certainly; but favour his extension and his acquisition of new markets in Asia (at the expense of England if need be) if you would see Capitalism hurry onward to its death.

It may be urged that our Irish nationality plays a large part in forming this conception of international politics here set forth. We do not plead guilty, but even if it were so the objection would be puerile. As Socialists we base our political policy on the class struggle of the workers, because we know that the self-interest of the workers lies our way. That the self-interest may sometimes be base does not affect the correctness of our position. In like manner the mere fact that the inherited (and often unreasoning) anti-British sentiment of a chauvinist Irish patriot impels him to the same conclusion as we arrived at as the result of our economic studies does not cause us to shrink from proclaiming our position, but rather leads us to rejoice that our propaganda is thus made all the easier by this none too common identity of aim established as a consequence of what we esteem the strong and irreconcilable hostility between English Imperialism and Socialism.

Dogma and Food

(December 1899)

At a meeting of the Sacred Heart Home in Dublin the other day a most powerful and impassioned appeal was made by the Archbishop of Dublin for funds to provide proper care and training for the Catholic children who, from the poverty and carelessness of their parents, frequently fall into the clutches of "proselytisers" who make their misery a weapon of warfare against their religion. We do not propose now, nor at any other time, to enter into the disputes of rival religions, but we do think that the occasion merits at least a passing notice on our part, helping as it does to illustrate the truth of our contention that the social question, or the bread and butter question, is the root question of all, and until it is settled no other question of fundamental importance can be grappled with in any but an incomplete and unsatisfactory manner.

For what is the position upon which the appeal for funds to carry on the charitable work of the Sacred Heart Home was based? That owing to the poverty-stricken condition of large masses of the people the Catholic faith of the children was at the mercy of those missionaries and other Protestant agencies who come with charitable contributions to the parents and make of their charity a means for obtaining control of the education and bodily person of the child.

Here then we have the statement clearly made that the manifold dangers against which we are so solemnly warned spring from POVERTY. Reasoning on this matter from the standpoint of a mere layman we would be inclined to say that the first line of attack along which the Archbishop should direct the forces of his eloquence, and the attention of the world in general, is that of poverty and the institutions which create it. If you destroy the social institutions which create poverty, if you lift the working class from their present position of economic dependence, and in so doing assure to all men and women a sufficiency of the good things in life in return for a moderate amount of labour, then the insidious work of the "souper" is ended and all religious denominations will require to stand or progress by their inherent truths alone.

But nowhere in all the passionate exhortations of our clerical leaders do we find this point ever noted; instead we are to have appeals for funds to be applied for the purpose of saving Catholic children from the temptations of "proselytisers;" and as said temptations usually take the form of food and raiment, to supply food, raiment, and if necessary, shelter through Catholic sources. In all this there is no question of whether it would be a subject worthy of consideration to consider what means should be taken to abolish the poverty which degrades the workers so much that they are ready to traffic in their children in such a manner.

Yet until this question is dealt with all the efforts of the Sacred Heart Home, and such-like institutions, will be of practically no avail in combatting such degradation. The place of the children rescued today will be filled tomorrow by the children of other parents hurled into the abyss of slum life and misery by the ceaseless working of our unjust social system. We on this journal, or in this party, are not allied, nor opposed to, any particular creed or Church – seeking the emancipation of the working class from the unholy trinity of Rent, Interest and Profit we require the aid of men of all religions and of none – but we consider it our duty to point out that if the speakers at the Sacred Heart Home at Drumcondra were really in earnest in their desire to save the children, they would find in the Municipal Programme of the Socialist Republican Party a plank, that of the Free Maintenance of Children, which, if applied in practice, would prevent effectually all that hopeless misery out of which such degrading incidents as those complained of spring.

But it is at all times more congenial to a certain class of minds to nibble at consequences rather than to strike boldly at the root of the evil; that, and the unpopularity sure to be the reward of the political party which, despising cheap methods of gaining sympathy, instead of whining over the sufferings of the poor, calls upon them to rebel against the oppressive institutions which cause it, explains why our public men in general are chary about touching a reform, be it ever so practical, which appeals to manhood rather than to wealth.

But all such admissions of timidity coupled with an admission of the degrading nature of capitalist society, such as that the assembled clerics treated us to on Monday last, only tend to confirm the faith of the Socialist Republican in that uncompromising course of action which rests all its hopes in the right arms and clear brains of the disinherited – the working class.

Let Us Free Ireland!

(1899)

Let us free Ireland! Never mind such base, carnal thoughts as concern work and wages, healthy homes, or lives unclouded by poverty.

Let us free Ireland! The rackrenting landlord; is he not also an Irishman, and wherefore should we hate him? Nay, let us not speak harshly of our brother – yea, even when he raises our rent.

Let us free Ireland! The profit-grinding capitalist, who robs us of three-fourths of the fruits of our labour, who sucks the very marrow of our bones when we are young, and then throws us out in the street, like a worn-out tool when we are grown prematurely old in his service, is he not an Irishman, and mayhap a patriot, and wherefore should we think harshly of him?

Let us free Ireland! "The land that bred and bore us." And the landlord who makes us pay for permission to live upon it. Whoop it up for liberty!

"Let us free Ireland," says the patriot who won't touch Socialism. Let us all join together and cr-r-rush the br-r-rutal Saxon. Let us all join together, says he, all classes and creeds. And, says the town worker, after we have crushed the Saxon and freed Ireland, what will we do? Oh, then you can go back to your slums, same as before. Whoop it up for liberty!

And, says the agricultural workers, after we have freed Ireland, what then? Oh, then you can go scraping around for the landlord's rent or the money-lenders' interest same as before. Whoop it up for liberty!

After Ireland is free, says the patriot who won't touch socialism, we will protect all classes, and if you won't pay your rent you will be evicted same as now. But the evicting party, under command of the sheriff, will wear green uniforms and the Harp without the Crown, and the warrant turning you out on the roadside will be stamped with the arms of the Irish Republic. Now, isn't that worth fighting for?

And when you cannot find employment, and, giving up the struggle of life in despair, enter the poorhouse, the band of the nearest regiment of the Irish army will escort you to the poorhouse door to the tune of St. Patrick's Day. Oh! It will be nice to live in those days!

"With the Green Flag floating o'er us" and an ever-increasing army of unemployed workers walking about under the Green Flag, wishing they had something to eat. Same as now! Whoop it up for liberty!

Now, my friend, I also am Irish, but I'm a bit more logical. The capitalist, I say, is a parasite on industry; as useless in the present stage of our industrial development as any other parasite in the animal or vegetable world is to the life of the animal or vegetable upon which it feeds.

The working class is the victim of this parasite – this human leech, and it is the duty and interest of the working class to use every means in its power to oust this parasite class from the position which enables it to thus prey upon the vitals of labour.

Therefore, I say, let us organise as a class to meet our masters and destroy their mastership; organise to drive them from their hold upon public life through their political power; organise to wrench from their robber clutch the land and workshops on and in which they enslave us; organise to cleanse our social life from the stain of social cannibalism, from the preying of man upon his fellow man.

Organise for a full, free and happy life FOR ALL OR FOR NONE.

Difficulties of Socialism

(1900)

In every discussion on the aims and objects of a Socialist Party some one is sure to bring up the objection that even if the Socialist Party were to conquer their opponents, and make an effort to establish their ideal as a political and social edifice, the difficulties which would arise out of the inability of the common people to understand the complexity of the social system they were called upon to administer, would infallibly produce the downfall of the new order. This objection is, it seems to us, rather far fetched in view of the circumstance that the majority of those who at the present day are entrusted with the work of organizing and administering the capitalist system are completely ignorant of every development of the system outside of their own particular sphere of employment.

It is not at all necessary that everyone, or even a very large number, of those engaged in labour should be able to give an intelligent account of the multifarious processes of production, nor yet that they should be qualified even to trace the passage of the commodities upon which they are employed through all their stages from the crudity of the raw material up to the perfection of the finished product as it eventually reaches the hands of the purchaser. It is only necessary that each worker should perform with due skill and scrupulosity his own allotted task; to the few required as organisers of industry may be left the work of adjusting and interlocking the parts. Even this latter function – formidable as it may look when thus baldly stated – may be reduced to a mere automatic function to be executed as a part of the routine work of a clerical staff.

Any person reflecting upon the mechanism of the capitalist system can readily perceive how little its most important arteries of commerce are dependent upon international organization, and how much upon the reciprocal action of the economic interests involved at first hand. Where the international organization of Socialism will indeed come into play it will come to smooth over and simplify many of the difficulties which are constantly arising under capitalism as a result of the clashing of personal interests. Hence the Socialist organization of industry will preserve the effectiveness due to the development of capitalism whilst entirely obviating the friction and disputes capitalist competition entails.

It is well also to remember the multitude of things which in civilised society we are all compelled to take upon trust at the word of others. It is safe to say that what is called 'progress', or civilisation, would be impossible were each individual in the community, or even a majority, to insist upon acquiring a complete theoretical and technical mastery of, say, each new application of Science to the needs of life before consenting to allow its use. There are few persons nowadays who would shrink from trusting themselves to railway trains, even although in all but complete ignorance of the mechanism of the steam engine, signal-boxes, points, and brakes; we have had gas in our houses, shops, and public buildings for several generations, but to this day the number of those who really understand the processes of gas production, storage, and distribution are extraordinarily few, yet that does not prevent us using it despite its well known poisonous and explosive nature. And so we might go on enumerating many things in daily use – the use of which involves risk to life – which are accepted and freely utilised by people at large without stopping to acquire a perfect knowledge of their active principle.

Much the same might be said of the pretended wonderful and mysterious results to be attained under Socialism – results too wonderful to be realised. In Socialism there is nothing so abnormal that its realization could exceed in strangeness things we see around us every day, and composedly accept with the greatest equanimity. In the proposition that the community can so arrange the work of production and distribution that plenty can be provided for every human being, there is nothing, in view of present day machinery, half so extraordinary as the fact that if a gentleman sitting down to dinner in Dublin sends a telegram to a friend in Australia that friend will have received said telegram before his Dublin correspondent could have finished the final course of his repast. The fact that people in Ireland were reading accounts of battles in South Africa, 7,000 miles off, while those battles were still in progress, is far more intrinsically wonderful than a system of society in which labour enjoys the product of its toil, and neither hereditary tyrants nor capitalist exploiters are tolerated.

If these stranger developments have been accepted whilst Socialism is still rejected, it is because the personal economic interests of the classes controlling the educative and governing forces of the world are in line with such developments, while the same personal economic interests of those classes are as directly opposed to Socialism. But the workers are in the majority, and their interests are in line with Socialism, which may, therefore, be realised as soon as they desire, and are resolute enough to put their desires into practice.

Home Thrusts

(June 1900)

The Irish Trades' Union Congress.

What have the working class of Ireland a right to expect from that gathering?

We know what we have received in the past – much talk, and many schemes whereby we might through combination better our lot as slaves, but never a suggestion on the point of how we might proceed to abolish our status as slaves, and elevate ourselves instead to the dignity of freemen.

For what, after all, are the various nostrums of Technical Education, Fair Wages Clause in Public Contracts, Amendments to Employers' Liability Acts, etc., what are they in essence but devices to modify the severity of the slave driver's lash, whilst still expressly recognising his right to apply the lash?

Take Technical Education. It is a scheme to provide the workers with increased knowledge of how to handle the tools with which they make a profit for their masters; it will not increase the wages of labour, but it will increase the number of really efficient workers seeking for employment, and competing against each other for wages.

If thorough Technical Education were made universal it would make skilled labour as plentiful as unskilled, and wages would be adjusted accordingly.

That is in any event the tendency introduced into modern industry by machinery; it is the inevitable result of the division of labour in the workshop, consequent upon the use of steam and electricity; but why trade unionists should imagine that it is their duty to spend valuable time in advocating reforms (?) which will destroy the distinction between skilled and unskilled labour, not by uplifting the latter but by degrading the former, we fail to understand.

It may be pleaded that as Technical Education would enable us to compete better with other nations it is a beneficent measure to that extent. Granted. But what is most urgently needed in Ireland is a frank discussion by organised labour of the basis and principles of the vile capitalist system which compels you to compete or die; to snatch the bread out of your neighbour's mouth, or starve yourself.

Technical Education will come. Of that be assured. The master class will introduce it in their own interests, my friends, so please use your time at your annual palaver at something a little more useful to yourselves and your class.

The Fair Wages Clause is somewhat more sensible, but does not deserve all the enconiums passed upon it. What is it at most? If carried out in its entirety it would ensure that the rate of wages paid in Government or Municipal service or contracts would be as high as the terms your trade unionists are able to force upon private employers. That is all!

Not a great lot to talk about, is it?

Especially in view of the fact that were you wise enough to think for yourselves, instead of blindly following the interested advice of the middle class on the one hand, or the muddle-headed traditions of English trade unionism on the other, you could carry your trade unionism into politics, and elect sufficient men of your own class to all public bodies, parliament included, to make these bodies the mouthpieces of your own interest, and their conditions of employment the ideal standard.

But that would be Socialism, you say. Oh no it wouldn't, not by a long shot. But if you had a majority of your representatives in the legislative chamber, and that majority proceeded to make capitalist property illegal, and to vote that all the land, mines, railways, canals, factories, shops, docks, and shipping belonged to the people of Ireland, and would in future be worked by them on a co-operative, democratic basis, that would be Socialism – and that would be freedom.

But as long as you recognise capitalist property, as long as you yield up to the master class the private property you of right possess in the product of your labour, and accept instead a fraction thereof in the shape of wages, then no matter how you may strive to limit the power of the master, he is master still – and you are but his slave.

Probably you won't talk about Socialism at the Congress. You will rather orate about the "dignity of labour," although well aware that the majority of delegates have to ask their masters' permission before they dare venture to attend the Congress.

Last year you resolved against the Overtaxation of Ireland, which only concerns our Irish upper class, who wanted your help against the English upper class. That was the result of your leaders being more anxious to get a word of praise from the Home Rule press than to know what they were talking about.

Last year your president said there was no antagonism between employers and employed. This year the same individual is in Dublin, busy organising the men of his trade who have been shamefully locked out by their masters. Does he still think there is no antagonism?

Consider, my trade unionist friends. We Irish are today the only working class in Europe who are not in revolt against the slavery of the capitalist system; we are the only people with whom the highest ambition in life is to get a good wage from their masters; we are the only people who have not risen intellectually to a conception of what life might be without masters; we are the only people, outside of England, who are trade unionists only in the shop, but become the veriest lackeys of our masters at the political ballot box; and we would all die for the freedom of our country, yet would continue that country in the hands of employers and landlords, who could at their will refuse us the right to live upon it.

Are there amongst the delegates to the Congress sufficient MEN to retrieve our name in the eyes of the world?

Then let them stand up for the only hope of the disinherited working class – the Socialist Republic.

Parliamentary Democracy

(September 1900)

Parliament is dissolved! By whom? By whom was Parliament elected? By the voters of Great Britain and Ireland. Was it then the voters of Great Britain and Ireland who called upon Parliament to dissolve? No, it was the Prime Minister of England, Lord Salisbury to wit, whom nobody elected and who is incapable under the laws of his country of being a parliamentary representative; it was this gentleman with whom lay the power of putting an end to the deliberations of Parliament and sending its members back to the ordeal of the hustings.

This ridiculous situation is highly illustrative of many anomalies and absurdities with which the English Constitution abounds. Eulogised by its supporters as the most perfect constitution yet evolved it is in reality so full of illogical and apparently impossible provisions and conditions that if presented to the reasoning mind as the basis of a workable constitution for a new country it would be laughed out of court as too ridiculous to consider.

Let us examine a few of its provisions in order that we may the more effectively contrast this parliamentary democracy with the democracy of the revolutionist. Parliament is elected by the voters of Great Britain and Ireland. When elected that party which counts the greatest number of followers is presumed to form the Cabinet as representing a majority of the electorate. But it by no means follows that a majority in the House represents a majority of the people. In many constituencies for instance where there are more than two candidates for a seat it frequently happens that although a candidate polls a larger vote than either of his opponents and so obtains the seat, yet he only represents a minority of the constituents as the vote cast for his two opponents if united would be much greater than his own. The cabinet formed out of the members of the party strongest numerically constitutes the government of the country and as such has full control of our destinies during its term of office. But the Cabinet is not elected by the Parliament, voted for by the people, nor chosen by its own party. The Cabinet is chosen by the gentleman chosen by the Sovereign as the leader of the strongest party. The gentleman so chosen after a consultation with the Queen (who perhaps detests both him and his party) selects certain of his own followers, and invests them with certain positions, and salaries, and so forms the Cabinet.

The Cabinet controls the government and practically dictates the laws, yet the Cabinet itself is unknown to the law and is not recognised by the Constitution. In fact the Cabinet is entirely destitute of any legal right to existence. Yet although outside the law and unknown to the Constitution it possesses the most fearful powers, such as the declaration of war, and can not be prevented by the elected representatives of the people from committing the nation to the perpetration of any crime it chooses. After the crime has been perpetrated Parliament can repudiate when it meets the acts of the Cabinet, but in the meanwhile nations may have been invaded, governments overturned, and territories devastated with fire and sword.

The powers of Parliament are also somewhat arbitrary and ill-defined. Every general election is fought on one or two main issues, and on these alone. It may be the Franchise, it may be Temperance, it may be Home Rule, or any other question, but when Parliament has received from the electors its mandate on that one question it arrogates to itself the right to rule and decide on every other question without the slightest reference to the wishes of the electorate.

If Parliament, elected to carry out the wishes of the electors on one question, chooses to act in a manner contrary to the wishes of the electors in a dozen other questions, the electors have no redress except to wait for another general election to give them the opportunity to return other gentlemen under similar conditions and with similar opportunities of evil-doing.

The democracy of Parliament is in short the democracy of Capitalism. Capitalism gives to the worker the right to choose his master, but insists that the fact of mastership shall remain unquestioned; Parliamentary Democracy gives to the worker the right to a voice in the selection of his rulers but insists that he shall bend as a subject to be ruled. The fundamental feature of both in their relation to the worker is that they imply his continued subjection to a ruling class once his choice of the personnel of the rulers is made.

But the freedom of the revolutionist will change the choice of rulers which we have to-day into the choice of administrators of laws voted upon directly by the people; and will also substitute for the choice of masters (capitalists) the appointment of reliable public servants under direct public control. That will mean true democracy – the industrial democracy of the Socialist Republic.

An Object Lesson

(December 1900)

On Wednesday November 28, there appeared in the Dublin newspapers an advertisement announcing the issue of shares in a new electrical syndicate, the "British Electrical Street Tramways, Limited". We do not suppose our readers are interested in that fact as probable subscribers for the shares of this company, but we nevertheless venture to draw their attention to the circumstance, because the advertisement in question was in itself an eloquent tribute to the validity of many of the points raised by Socialists in their criticism of the capitalist system. The Syndicate is formed, the advertisement tells us, "to construct and work lines of electric railways and tramways licensed by special Acts of Parliament, or by Municipal or other authorities, and to extend the service of traction vehicles in large towns".

Here we have a proposal by a number of rich men to engage in the business of constructing and working electric trams, etc, in any town of Great Britain and Ireland where they can procure permission to do so, and coupled with the proposal is an estimate of the large profits to be acquired by such a proceeding – to be acquired by whoever purchases shares in this company, even though the person so purchasing may be entirely ignorant of all that pertains to electric traction, or unable to visit any of the towns where the profits are to be earned. Tender-hearted humanitarians and benevolent persons generally, aghast at the miseries of the workers but loth to relinquish their belief in the institution of private property, are never tired of proclaiming that the cure-all for those miseries is to be found in the cultivation of feelings of friendship between capitalists and their workers. They affirm that strikes, lock-outs, and industrial disputes of all kinds would be rendered impossible if the employers and employed were only to meet and know each other better.

To this contention Socialists have always replied that the development of modern industry renders impossible any such rapprochement between the classes; that the employer is no longer a person but a thing – a company; that, the shares of said company being saleable on the market, the personality of the shareholder is of a fleeting character, and that consequently the possibility of human, personal, intercourse between master and man is fast being destroyed by the inevitable tendency of industry to fall into the hands of companies, and of companies to form combinations or trusts. The man who holds shares in companies situated a hundred or a thousand miles distant from his home cannot have a personal regard for the employees who earn his dividends, and the employees cannot be expected to remember in their prayers shareholders whose very names are unknown to them. The fact of this company offering its shares promiscuously to all who choose to buy, and proposing to exploit the needs of towns wherever possible, proves this Socialist contention to be absolutely correct. How can anyone believe that the monied people rushing to buy these shares could be brought to regard as men and brothers the unfortunate workmen whose labours they hope to profit by?

One other and more important point is brought out by this advertisement, viz., that the private capitalist is no longer necessary. Apologists for capitalism claim that the profits of the capitalist are the reward of his brains and skill in organising; that without the brains and organising genius of the capitalist industry would be impossible. But here we observe in this case, as in the case of all capitalist companies, that the profits are to be reaped by people who bring neither brains, skill, nor even technical knowledge to the work – who bring nothing but cash to purchase the brains and muscle of other men.

All the organising and managerial functions of the company will be performed by experts hired for the purpose. These experts need have no interest in the company other than their salaries. It is obvious, then, that when private capitalist companies can hire servants to perform the brain work necessary for their schemes, the same class of persons could be hired, if need be, by the public bodies, state or municipal, to perform the same functions in the service of, and for the interest of, the entire community.

By the hiring of salaried managers the capitalist class abandon all right to use the plea that the community could not progress without their aid; since personal supervision and direction by the capitalist himself is not required, the public bodies who represent the community can safely undertake the ownership and control of all the work of production and distribution; and solve the problem of organising skill and genius by the same method as that employed by the capitalist class today, viz., by hiring technical experts to organise and direct.

Thus the first step in the Socialist organisation of industry is illustrated by the last step in capitalist organisation. The capitalist having voluntarily abdicated his personal supervision, in his own interest, must now abdicate his personal ownership, in the general interest.

Unpatriotic?

(May 1903)

In every country of the earth in which Socialism has taken root its advocates meet with the objection that their doctrines are 'unpatriotic', that Socialism is a foreign idea. Whether it be in Ireland, Germany, France, America, England, Russia, Italy or any other country we find the enemies of Socialism harping upon this one theme, the unpatriotic character of the Socialist movement. It is fitting, therefore, that we should examine and analyse this theory in order that we may find out upon what it is founded, how it is that in countries so widely separated the Socialist movement meets with an almost identical objection – in conservative Ireland as in cosmopolitan America.

We need not go far in our analysis. It is an axiom accepted by all Socialists that the ruling class industrially will always be the ruling class politically, and will also dominate in all other walks of life and fields of thought.

That until the epoch of revolution arrives the interests of the class who hold the dominant machinery of production will colour and mould the entire thought and institutions of society at large; making whatever serves such interests appear as 'patriotic', 'native' and thoroughly 'Irish' or 'American' or whatever the nationality of the possessing class may be. And in like manner stamping as 'foreign', 'unpatriotic', 'un-Irish' or 'un-American' everything that savours of danger to that possessing class. In other words the possessing class always and everywhere arrogates to itself an exclusive right to be considered the Nation, and basing itself upon that right to insist that the laws of the land should be in its hands to frame and administer in its own interests, which, it pleasantly informs us, are the highest interests of the nation.

This is a characteristic of the propertied classes everywhere, even where they are not a ruling class. The Land League agitation in Ireland, and in a lesser degree the present Land agitation, exemplified this trait. The Land League agitation centred round the fight of the tenant farmers for better terms for their holdings. It was primarily a contest betwixt tenant and landlord.

The agricultural labourer had no concern in it, indeed he invariably got better terms from the landlord than the tenant farmer; the urban population had no interests directly at stake, town workers were not considered in Land Bills; all the mercantile, industrial and professional classes knew they would be left outside the scope of the settlement between landlord and tenant should one be arrived at, yet, the tenant farmers being organised politically and industrially, and above all being class-conscious, that is to say conscious of the identity of their class interests, succeeded in impressing the character of their movement upon the whole life of Ireland.

Every farmer's grievance became an Irish national grievance, every farmer refusing to pay rent was idealised as a patriot battling, not for his own purse, but for his country, every farmer evicted was acclaimed as a martyr for his country; if a man took an evicted farm he was not merely a landgrabber or scab on his class, he was a traitor to 'Ireland', and every person who spoke to him, or helped to feed, clothe or shelter him was also an enemy to Ireland, a traitor to his native land, a Judas or a Diarmuid Mac Murchadha. Thus the tenant farmers dominated the thought of the country and made the fight of their own class for its rights identical with the idea of Irish patriotism.

Now we are not pointing this fact out in order to denounce it. On the contrary we consider the farmers acted wisely in their own interests. But we do point it out in order to emphasise our contention that any particular act or political doctrine is patriotic or unpatriotic in the exact proportion in which it serves the interests of the class who for the time being hold political power. The Farmers of Ireland denounced as unpatriotic everything that failed to serve their class interests, including even the labourer's demand for a cottage; let the Working Class of Ireland follow their lead and test the sincerity of every man's patriotism by his devotion to the interests of Labour. In the eyes of the farmer no wagging of green flags could make a landgrabber a patriot: let the Workers apply the same test and brand as enemies to Ireland all who believe in the subjection of Labour to Capital – brand as traitors to this country all who live by skinning Irish Labour.

For the working class of the world the lesson is also plain. In every country Socialism is foreign, is unpatriotic, and will continue so until the Working Class embracing it as their salvation make Socialism the dominant political force.

Then the interests of the Working Class will be in the ascendant and every man's patriotism will be gauged by his services and devotion to these interests, thus Socialism will be patriotic and native everywhere, and the advocates of Capitalistic property will be the unpatriotic ones.

By their aggressiveness and intolerance the possessing classes erect the principles of their capitalist supremacy into the dignity of national safeguards; according as the Working Class infuses into its political organisation the same aggressiveness and intolerance will it command the success it deserves, and make the Socialist the only good and loyal citizen.

Declaration of Principles of the Irish Socialist Federation

(1908)

New York, January 1908

The Irish Socialist Federation is composed of members of the Irish race in America, and is organised to assist the revolutionary working-class movement in Ireland by a dissemination of its literature, to educate the working-class Irish of this country into a knowledge of Socialist principles and to prepare them to co-operate with the workers of all other races, colours and nationalities in the emancipation of labour.

It affirms its belief that political and social freedom are not two separate and unrelated ideas, but are two sides of the one great principle, each being incomplete without the other.

The course of society politically has been from warring but democratic tribes within each nation to a united government under an absolutely undemocratic monarchy. Within this monarchy again developed revolts against its power, revolts at first seeking to limit its prerogatives only, then demanding the inclusion of certain classes in the governing power, then demanding the right of the subject to criticise and control the power of the monarch, and finally, in the most advanced countries, this movement culminated in the total abolition of the monarchial institution and the transformation of the subject into the citizen.

In industry a corresponding development has taken place. The independent producer, owning his own tools and knowing no master, has given way before the more effective productive powers of huge capital, concentrated in the hands of the great capitalist. The latter, recognising no rights in his workers, ruled as an absolute monarch in his factory. But within the realm of capital developed a revolt against the power of the capitalist. This revolt, taking the form of trade unionism, has pursued in the industrial field the same line of development as the movement for political freedom has pursued in the sphere of national government. It first contented itself with protests against excessive exactions, against all undue stretchings of the power of the capitalist, then its efforts broadened out to demands for restrictions upon the absolute character of such power, i.e., by claiming for trade unions the right to make rules for the workers in the workshop; then it sought still further to curb the capitalist's power by shortening the working day and so limiting the period during which the toiler may be exploited. Finally, it seeks by Boards of Arbitration to establish an equivalent in the industrial world for that compromise in the political world by which, in constitutional countries, the monarch retains his position by granting a parliament to divide with him the duties of governing, and so hides while securing his power. And as in the political history of the race, the logical development of progress was found in the abolition of the institution of monarchy and not in its mere restriction, so in industrial history the culminating point to which all efforts must at last converge lies in the abolition of the capitalist class and not in the mere restriction of its power.

It recognises in all past history a preparation for this achievement, and in the industrial tendencies of today it hails the workings out of those laws of human progress which bring that object within our reach.

The concentration of capital in the form of trusts simplifies the task we propose that society shall undertake and the industrial organisation of labour resultant therefrom drills and prepares the force necessary to its accomplishment.

As today the organised power of the State theoretically guarantees to every individual his political rights, so in the Socialist Republic the power and productive forces of organised society will stand between every individual and want, guaranteeing that right to life without which all other rights are but mockery.

The Irish Socialist Federation, recognising these two phases of human development, pledges its members to fealty to the principles resultant therefrom, politically rejecting the domination of nation over nation as of man over man; it on the field of Irish politics is organised against every party recognising British rule in Ireland in any form or manner, in all its moods and modifications; and as the final solution of the Irish, as of every other struggle for freedom, it seeks the Workers' Republic – the administration of all the land and instruments of labour, all social property in which all shall be co-heirs and owners.

A Political Party of the Workers

(January 1908)

With the advent of an Irish Socialist paper in the labor movement of America will come of necessity a host of questions and questioners upon the attitude of the proprietors of that paper toward the political parties at present in the field for Socialism. Such questions are unavoidable, and it is therefore best that they be faced at once at the outset without delay or equivocation.

Let it be noted therefore that the *Harp* is the official organ of the Irish Socialist Federation in America, and that that body was founded with the intention, expressed and desired, of spreading the light of Socialism amongst the working class Irish in this country, and that, recognizing that the existence of two political parties of Socialism has had in the past and has now a confusing effect upon the minds of the American working class, the founders of the Federation recognized that it would be worse than folly to make allegiance to one or the other of these political divisions a test of membership in the newly founded camp of Irish Socialists in America. The Federation is not founded for political action, it is founded for propaganda; it is not in existence to fashion a political machine, it is in existence to present Socialism as a historical development from capitalism and as the only remedy for the wage slavery of the workers. The task of presenting the Socialist side as against the side of the capitalists, with all their powerful allies and weapons, is a big enough job for us without also taking part in the campaigns of slander which form the stock in trade of the American Socialists when they condescend to refer to each other. In their mutual recriminations many wrong things have been said, many right things have been wrongly said, and we are convinced that if American Socialists in general had been more solicitous in finding and emphasizing the points they had in common, and less eager to stretch the importance of the points on which they differed, a great party – great in unity in essentials, great in numbers – might long ere this have been built up in America. And until that party does appear the ISF will confine its work to the making of Socialists; let its recruits when made choose their own political affiliations.

But, it may be said, since the Irish comrades deplore the existing division, have they no suggestion to offer whereby it may be ended? Is it not certain that as you make recruits to Socialism, and those recruits choose their own political affiliations, that in course of time their differing choices will result in bringing into the Federation the disputes which divide Socialists outside? That is true, and therefore it is to our interest as well as in conformity with our desires to find some common ground upon which in our opinion earnest revolutionary Socialists could meet to combine their forces in battle with the common enemy.

The common ground of action we favor is one for which a strong sentiment already exists in the rank and file of both existing parties. It has been adopted and endorsed by practically all the non-English-using federations of Socialists in America, and has therefore strong organized forces already behind it, and it would, as a magnet, draw unto itself all the true proletarian Socialists and weld them into an irresistible force. A common ground of action to be effectual for its purpose cannot emanate from either SP or SLP; it cannot be furnished by unity conferences, no matter how earnest the conferees are; the ghost of all the hatreds and jealousies aroused by the past years of strife will perpetually rise between the most united unity conference and the realization of its hopes, and, finally, it cannot be realized by an amalgamation of the existing parties. There are too many leaders, save the mark! Too many 'saviors of the working class' whose reputations have been built upon disunion; too many petty personal ambitions which might be endangered did the rank and file have an opportunity to know and understand one another; and too much fear that a general reunion might mean a general housecleaning, and the consequent dumping upon the garbage heap of many great lights whose personal predominance is dearer to them than the power of the movement. Some men in the Socialist movement on both sides would rather have a party of ten men who unquestioningly accepted their dictum and called their blind faith 'democracy' than a party of half a million whose component elements dared to think and act for themselves. Unquestionably the realization of unity must have as its necessary concomitant the acceptance of the fact that the interests of the movement are greater than and superior to the prejudices or rivalries of its leaders.

What and where, then, is this common ground we have spoken of? As we have already stated, the ISF is pledged to no political party, but this neutrality on the political field is not extended to the economic. There, we believe, an assumption of neutrality would be a crime on our part. Between, on the one hand, the new economic organization, the Industrial Workers of the World, which prepares and organizes the administrative framework of society in the future, and at the same time furnishes the only effective method of resistance against present-day encroachments of the master class, and on the other hand the old-style pure and simple trade unionism of the AF of L with its system of dividing the working class and its professed belief in the identity of interests between Capital and Labor, between these two economic organizations our choice is as plain and unmistakable as between Socialism and Capitalism; indeed, it is the same proposition presented in different terms. And as we believe that all working class Socialists must realize that their place is in the only real economic organization truly worthy of the name of union, the IWW, so we believe that the same body has it in its power to solve the problem of Socialist unity. On the day that the IWW launches its own political party it will put an end to all excuse for two Socialist parties and open the way for a real and effective unification of the revolutionary forces. To it will flock all the real proletarians, all the loyal-hearted working class whom distrust and suspicion have so long kept divided: it will be the real Political Party of the Workers – the weapon by which the working class will register the decrees which its economic army must and shall enforce.

We do not say this will end forever all fear of the existence of two parties calling themselves Socialists, but it will end all possibilty of two revolutionary Socialist parties claiming the allegiance of the working class at the same moment. Compromisers and schemers will still erect parties to serve their personal ends and satiate their lust for being worshipped; intellectual mannikins will still perch themselves upon the shoulders of the workers and imagining their high altitude is the result of transcendent ability on their part will call the world to witness how great they are; but they will be deprived of their power to delude the real revolutionist by the simple fact of the existence of a political party of Socialists dominated by and resting upon the economic movement of the working class.

This is our hope, our proposed solution of the problem of divided forces, and on the day that that hope is consummated if anyone looks around for the class-conscious Irish workers he will, we believe, find them alert and determined at the head of the fighters.

Sinn Féin And Socialism

(April 1908)

Sinn Féin.

That is a good name for the new Irish movement of which we hear so much nowadays. Sinn Féin, or in English, Ourselves.

It is a good name and a good motto. The first essential for the success of any party, or of any movement, is that it should believe it carries within its own bosom all the material requisite to achieve its destiny. The moment any organization ceases to believe in the sufficiency of its own powers, the moment its membership begin to put their trust in powers not their own, in that moment that party or that organization enters on its decline.

It has been so with Ireland, it is so with the non-Socialist Working Class.

For over a hundred years Ireland has looked outside her own shores for the means of her redemption. For over a hundred years Ireland through her 'constitutional agitators' has centered her hopes upon the possibility of melting the heart or appealing to the sense of justice of her oppressors. In vain! England – the British Empire, was and is the bourgeoisie personified, the incarnate beast of capitalist property, and her heart was as tender as that of the tiger when he feels his victim helpless in his claws; her sense of justice was as acute as that of the same beast of prey when his jaws are wet with the warm blood of the feast.

For over a hundred years the majority of the Irish people begged for justice, and when ever and anon the hot blood of the best of her children would rise in rebellion at this mendicant posture Ireland turned her face from them and asked the enemy to forgive them.

When her rebel sons and daughters were dead, hunted, imprisoned, hanged or exiled she would weep for them, pray for them, sigh for them, cry for them, and when they were long enough out of the way, erect monuments to them.

But as long as they were virile, active and aggressive, Ireland regarded them only as disturbers who gave the country a bad name.

Not that Ireland was or is alone in that respect. To be execrated when living and deified when dead has been the experience of all champions of Freedom in all the countries and ages of the earth.

This attitude, whether it is exhibited by an oppressed nation or by an oppressed class, is the direct outcome of that frame of mind in either which teaches them to look outside their own ranks for the impulse towards emancipation.

To believe that someone else than the slave is going to free the slave makes the slave impatient and intolerant of every effort at self-liberation on the part of his fellow bondsmen.

Now the course of action implied in the name Sinn Féin, is the reverse of all that. It teaches the Irish people to rely upon themselves, and upon themselves alone, and teaches them also that dependence upon forces outside themselves is emasculating in its tendency, and has been, and will ever be disastrous in its results.

So far, so good. That is a part of Sinn Féinism I am most heartily in agreement with, and indeed with the spirit of Sinn Féin every thinking Irishman who knows anything about the history of his country must concur.

Even on the question of the Irish language, Gaelic, a question on which most Socialists are prone to stumble, I am heartily in accord. I do believe in the necessity, and indeed in the inevitability, of a universal language, but I do not believe it will be brought about, or even hastened, by smaller races or nations consenting to the extinction of their language. Such a course of action, or rather of slavish inaction, would not hasten the day of a universal language, but would rather lead to the intensification of the struggle for mastery between the languages of the greater powers.

On the other hand a large number of small communities speaking different tongues, are more likely to agree upon a common language as a common means of communication than a small number of great empires, each jealous of its own power and seeking its own supremacy.

I have heard some doctrinaire Socialists arguing that Socialists should not sympathize with oppressed nationalities, or with nationalities resisting conquest. They argue that the sooner these nationalities are suppressed the better, as it will be easier to conquer political power in a few big empires than in a number of small states. This is the language argument over again.

It is fallacious in both cases. It is even more fallacious in the case of nationalities than in the case of languages, because the emancipation of the Working Class will function more through the economic power than through the political state. The first act of the workers will be through their economic organizations seizing the organized industries; the last act the conquest of political power.

In this the working class will, as they needs must, follow in the lines traversed by the capitalist revolutions of Cromwellian England, of Colonial and Revolutionary America, of Republican France, in each of whom the capitalist class had developed their economic power before they raised the banner of political revolt.

The Working Class in their turn must perfect their economic organizations, and when such organizations are in a position to control, seize and operate the industries they will find their political power equal to the task.

But the preparatory work of the revolutionary campaign must lie in the daily and hourly struggles in the workshop, the daily and hourly perfectioning of the industrial organization.

And these two factors for Freedom take no heed to political frontiers, nor to the demarcations of political states. They march side by side with the capitalist; where capitalism brings its machinery it brings the rebels against itself, and all its governments and all its armies can establish no frontier the revolutionary idea cannot pass.

Let the great truth be firmly fixed in your mind that the struggle for the conquest of the political state of the capitalist is not the battle, it is only the echo of the battle. The real battle is being fought out, and will be fought out, on the industrial field.

Because of this and other reasons the doctrinaire Socialists are wrong in this as in the rest of their arguments. It is not necessary that Irish Socialists should hostilise those who are working for the Gaelic language, nor whoop it up for territorial aggrandizement of any nation. Therefore in this we can wish the Sinn Féiners, good luck.

Besides, it is well to remember that nations which submit to conquest or races which abandon their language in favor of that of an oppressor do so, not because of altruistic motives, or because of a love of the brotherhood of man, but from a slavish and cringing spirit.

From a spirit which cannot exist side by side with the revolutionary idea.

This was amply evidenced in Ireland by the attitude of the Irish people towards their language.

For six hundred years the English strove to suppress that mark of the distinct character of the Gael – their language, and failed. But in one generation the politicians did what England had failed to do.

The great Daniel O'Connell, the so-called liberator, conducted his meetings entirely in English. When addressing meetings in Connaught where in his time everybody spoke Gaelic, and over 75 per cent of the people nothing else but Gaelic, O'Connell spoke exclusively in English. He thus conveyed to the simple people the impression that Gaelic was something to be ashamed of – something fit only for ignorant people. He pursued the same course all over Ireland.

As a result of this and similar actions the simple people turned their backs upon their own language, and began to ape 'the gentry'. It was the beginning of the reign of the toady, and the crawler, the seáinín and the slave.

The agitator for revenue came into power in the land.

It is not ancient history, but the history of yesterday that old Irish men and women would speak Irish to each other in the presence of their children, but if they caught son or daughter using the language the unfortunate child would receive a cuff on the ear accompanied with the adjuration:

"Speak English, you rascal; speak English like a gintleman!"

It is freely stated in Ireland that when the Protestant evangelizers, soupers they call them at home, issued tracts and Bibles in Irish in order to help the work of proselytizing, the Catholic priesthood took advantage of the incident to warn their flocks against reading all literature in Gaelic. Thus still further discrediting the language.

I can not conceive of a Socialist hesitating in his choice between a policy resulting in such self-abasement, and a policy of defiant self-reliance, and confident trust in a people's own power of self-emancipation by a people.

But it is in many of the arguments used by the Sinn Féin speakers that the possibility, nay, the certainty of friction between the Irish Socialist and the adherents of Sinn Féin is likely to arise. Some of the arguments are as ridiculous as the principle itself is reasonable.

Thus the Sinn Féin body of the Argentine Republic, as recorded in the Gaelic American, states that Sinn Féin demands freedom for Ireland on the basis of the Act of Renunciation in 1782. This is absurd. The act by which the English Parliament renounced the right to make laws binding on Ireland left untouched the power of oppression, political and economic.

The fight which ended with the Act of Union in 1800 was not a fight for freedom, it was a fight to decide whether the English governing classes or the Irish governing classes should have the biggest share of the plunder of the Irish worker. Whichever side won made no difference to the worker; he was skinned, anyway.

As a cold matter of fact all talk about the "restoration of our native Parliament" is misreading history. Ireland never had an Irish Parliament – a Parliament representative of the Irish people. The assembly called by the name of an Irish Parliament was in reality as alien to the Irish people as the Council of the Governor-General of India is alien to the Indian people. And some of the laws passed by our so-called native Parliament against the poor Irish peasantry were absolutely revolting in their ferocity and class vindictiveness.

Irish workers will not enthuse worth a cent over a proposal to re-introduce the status of 1782. To paraphrase Fintan Lalor, and I would recommend all thinking Irish workers, men and women, to read Fintan Lalor's masterly argument upon this subject, (price five cents, from the *Harp* office). "This is not 1782, this is 1908," and every political or social movement which hopes for success must express itself in terms of present conditions, or on the lines of future developments.

Of a like character are the arguments based upon the achievement of Hungary. As we all know the methods adopted by Hungary to reconquer its Parliament from Austria are the trite illustrations of the Sinn Féin orators. In fact during the early stages of the movement in Ireland before the felicitous name of Sinn Féin was coined the ideas as promulgated got the name of 'the Hungary system'.

I remember one critic declaring that "the Hungary system was only fit for hungry men."

When we remember that Hungary is one of the European countries sending the greatest stream of emigrants annually to America, that the overwhelming majority of the producing classes in Hungary are denied the right to vote by the possessing classes who dominate their Parliament, that the misery of the town and country workers is so great that the country is in a chronic state of rebellion and unrest, and that the military and armed police are more often employed to suppress peaceable demonstrations in Hungary than they are in Ireland, we are inclined to wonder if our Sinn Féin orators know these things, or are they only presuming upon the ignorance of the Irish Workers.

Let them advocate their proposals upon the inherent merits of those proposals and they will avoid much criticism; otherwise they will provoke it.

Sinn Féin. Ourselves. I wonder how long it will be until the Working Class realize the full significance of that principle! How long it will be until the Workers realize that the Socialist movement is a movement of the Working Class, and how long until the Socialists realize that the place of every other class in the movement is and must be a subordinate one.

How long it will be until the Socialists realize the folly and inconsistency of preaching to the Workers that the emancipation of the Working Class must be the act of the workers themselves, and yet presenting to those workers the sight of every important position in the party occupied by men not of the Working Class.

We will get the Workers to have trust in their own power to achieve their own emancipation when we demonstrate our belief that there is no task incidental to that end that a worker can not accomplish; when we train the workers to look inward upon their own class for everything required, to have confidence in the ability of their own class to fill every position in the revolutionary army; when, in short, we of the Socialist Working Class take to heart the full meaning of the term Sinn Féin, Ourselves, and apply it to the work of Industrial Reconstruction, the era of the strutters and poseurs will end and we will realize at last what was meant by Marx when he spoke of the revolt of those who

Have Nothing to Lose but their Chains.

Industrial Unionism and Constructive Socialism

(1908)

"There is not a Socialist in the world today who can indicate with any degree of clearness how we can bring about the co-operative commonwealth except along the lines suggested by industrial organization of the workers."

"Political institutions are not adapted to the administration of industry. Only industrial organizations are adapted to the administration of a co-operative commonwealth that we are working for. Only the industrial form of organization offers us even a theoretical constructive Socialist programme. There is no constructive Socialism except in the industrial field."

The above extracts from the speech of Delegate Stirton, editor of the *Wage Slave*, of Hancock, Michigan, so well embody my ideas upon this matter that I have thought well to take them as a text for an article in explanation of the structural form of Socialist society. In a previous chapter I have analysed the weakness of the craft or trade union form of organization alike as a weapon of defence against the capitalist class in everyday conflict on the economic field, and as a generator of class consciousness on the political field, and pointed out the greater effectiveness for both purposes of an industrial form of organization.

Organizing Constructively

"In the present article I desire to show how they who are engaged in building up industrial organizations for the practical purpose of today are at the same time preparing the framework of the society of the future. It is the realization of that feat that indeed marks the emergence of Socialism as a revolutionary force from the critical to the positive stage. Time was when Socialists, if asked how society would be organized under Socialism, replied invariably, and airily, that such things would be left to the future to decide. The fact was that they had not considered the matter, but the development of the Trust and Organized Capital in general, making imperative the Industrial Organizations of Labour on similar lines, has provided us with an answer at once more complete to ourselves and more satisfying to our questioners."

Now to analyse briefly the logical consequences of the position embodied in the above quotation.

"Political institutions are not adapted to the administration of industry."

Here is a statement that no Socialist with a clear knowledge of the essentials of his doctrine can dispute. The political institutions of today are simply the coercive forces of capitalist society they have grown up out of, and are based upon, territorial divisions of power in the hands of the ruling class in past ages, and were carried over into capitalist society to suit the needs of the capitalist class when that class overthrew the dominion of its predecessors.

The Old Order and the New

The delegation of the function of government into the hands of representatives elected from certain districts, States or territories, represents no real natural division suited to the requirements of modern society, but is a survival from a time when territorial influences were more potent in the world than industrial influences, and for that reason is totally unsuited to the needs of the new social order, which must be based upon industry.

The Socialist thinker, when he paints the structural form of the new social order, does not imagine an industrial system directed or ruled by a body of men or women elected from an indiscriminate mass of residents within given districts, said residents working at a heterogeneous collection of trades and industries. To give the ruling, controlling, and directing of industry into the hands of such a body would be too utterly foolish.

What the Socialist does realize is that under a social democratic form of society the administration of affairs will be in the hands of representatives of the various industries of the nation; that the workers in the shops and factories will organize themselves into unions, each union comprising all the workers at a given industry; that said union will democratically control the workshop life of its own industry, electing all foremen etc., and regulating the routine of labour in that industry in subordination to the needs of society in general, to the needs of its allied trades, and to the departments of industry to which it belongs; that representatives elected from these various departments of industry will meet and form the industrial administration or national government of the country.

Begin in the Workshop

In short, social democracy, as its name implies, is the application to industry, or to the social life of the nation, of the fundamental principles of democracy. Such application will necessarily have to begin in the workshop, and proceed logically and consecutively upward through all the grades of industrial organization until it reaches the culminating point of national executive power and direction. In other words, social democracy must proceed from the bottom upward, whereas capitalist political society is organized from above downward.

Social democracy will be administered by a committee of experts elected from the industries and professions of the land; capitalist society is governed by representatives elected from districts, and is based upon territorial division.

The local and national governing, or rather administrative, bodies of Socialists will approach every question with impartial minds, armed with the fullest expert knowledge born of experience; the governing bodies of capitalist society have to call in an expensive professional expert to instruct them on every technical question, and know that the impartiality of said expert varies with, and depends upon, the size of his fee.

No 'Servile State'

It will be seen that this conception of Socialism destroys at one blow all the fears of a bureaucratic State, ruling and ordering the lives of every individual from above, and thus gives assurance that the social order of the future will be an extension of the freedom of the individual, and not the suppression of it. In short, it blends the fullest democratic control with the most absolute expert supervision, something unthinkable of any society built upon the political State.

To focus the idea properly in your mind you have but to realize how industry today transcends all limitations of territory and leaps across rivers, mountains and continents; then you can understand how impossible it would be to apply to such far-reaching intricate enterprises the principle of democratic control by the workers through the medium of political territorial divisions.

Under Socialism, States, territories, or provinces will exist only as geographical expressions, and have no existence as sources of governmental power, though they may be seats of administrative bodies.

Now, having grasped the idea that the administrative force of the Socialist republic of the future will function through unions industrially organized, that the principle of democratic control will operate through the workers correctly organized in such industrial unions, and that the political territorial State of capitalist society will have no place or function under Socialism, you will at once grasp the full truth embodied in the words of this member of the Socialist Party whom I have just quoted, that "only the industrial form of organization offers us even a theoretical constructive Socialist programme."

The Political State and its Uses

To some minds constructive Socialism is embodied in the work of our representatives on the various public bodies to which they have been elected. The various measures against the evils of capitalist property brought forward by, or as a result of, the agitation of Socialist representatives on legislative bodies are figured as being of the nature of constructive Socialism.

As we have shown, the political State of capitalism has no place under Socialism; therefore, measures which aim to place industries in the hands of, or under the control of, such a political State are in no sense steps towards that ideal; they are but useful measures to restrict the greed of capitalism and to familiarize the workers with the conception of common ownership. This latter is, indeed, their chief function.

But the enrolment of the workers in unions patterned closely after the structure of modem industries, and following the organic lines of industrial development, is par excellence the swiftest, safest, and most peaceful form of constructive work the Socialist can engage in. It prepares within the framework of capitalist society the working forms of the Socialist republic, and thus, while increasing the resisting power of the worker against present encroachments of the capitalist class, it familiarizes him with the idea that the union he is helping to build up is destined to supplant that class in the control of the industry in which he is employed.

The Union Can Build Freedom

The power of this idea to transform the dry detail work of trade union organization into the constructive work of revolutionary Socialism, and thus make of the unimaginative trade unionist a potent factor in the launching of a new system of society, cannot be overestimated. It invests the sordid details of the daily incidents of the class struggle with a new and beautiful meaning, and presents them in their true light as skirmishes between the two opposing armies of light and darkness.

In the light of this principle of industrial unionism every fresh shop or factory organized under its banner is a fort wrenched from the control of the capitalist class and manned with the soldiers of the revolution to be held by them for the workers.

On the day that the political and economic forces of Labour finally break with capitalist society and proclaim the Workers' Republic, these shops and factories so manned by industrial unionists will be taken charge of by the workers there employed, and force and effectiveness be thus given to that proclamation. Then and thus the new society will spring into existence, ready equipped to perform all the useful functions of its predecessor.

Sinn Fein, Socialism and the Nation

(January 1909)

In a recent issue of *The Peasant*, a correspondent, 'Cairbre,' in the midst of a very fair and reasonable article on Sinn Fein and Socialism, says: "A rapprochement between Sinn Feinism and Socialism is highly desirable." To this I desire to say a fervent "Amen," and to follow up in my prayer with a suggestion which may help in realising such a desirable consummation. Always presupposing that the rapprochement is desired between Sinn Feiners who sympathise with Socialism and not merely with those who see no further than "the Constitution of '82," on the one hand, and Socialists who realise that a Socialist movement must rest upon and draw its inspiration from the historical and actual conditions of the country in which it functions and not merely lose themselves in an abstract 'internationalism' (which has no relation to the real internationalism of the Socialist movement), on the other.

But, first, it would be as well to state some of the difficulties in the way in order that we may shape our course in order to avoid them.

Sinn Fein has two sides – its economic teaching and its philosophy of self-reliance. With its economic teaching, as expounded by my friend Mr. Arthur Griffith in his adoption of the doctrines of Frederick List, Socialists have no sympathy, as it appeals only to those who measure a nation's prosperity by the volume of wealth produced in a country, instead of by the distribution of that wealth amongst the inhabitants. According to that definition, Ireland in 1847 was a prosperous country because it exported food, whereas Denmark was comparatively unprosperous because it exported little. But with that part of Sinn Fein which teaches that Ireland must rely upon itself, respect her own traditions, know her own history, preserve her own language and literature without prejudice to, or denial of, the worth in the language or literature of other people, stand erect in her own worth and claim to be appraised for her own intrinsic value, and not as part of the wheels and cogs of the imperial system of another people – with that side of Sinn Fein Socialists may sympathise; and, indeed, as a cold matter of fact, those doctrines were preached in Dublin by the Irish Socialist Republican Party from 1896 onward, before the Sinn Fein movement was founded.

The first side of Sinn Fein necessarily excludes the Socialists; the second does not. The first rests upon a capitalist conception of progress; the second is a gateway by which Ireland may enter into the intellectual domain which Socialism has made its own by its spiritual affinity with all the world-wide forces making for social freedom.

Socialists are also somewhat divided in their ideas as to what is a proper course in a country like Ireland. One set, observing that those who talk loudest about 'Ireland a Nation' are often the most merciless grinders of the faces of the poor, fly off to the extreme limit of hostility to Nationalism and, whilst opposed to oppression at all times, are also opposed to national revolt for national independence.

Another, principally recruited amongst the workers in the towns of North-East Ulster, have been weaned by Socialist ideas and industrial disputes from the leadership of Tory and Orange landlords and capitalists; but as they are offered practical measures of relief from capitalist oppression by the English Independent Labour Party, and offered nothing but a green flag by Irish Nationalism, they naturally go where they imagine relief will come from. Thus their social discontent is lost to the Irish cause. These men see that the workers shot down last winter in Belfast were not shot down in the interests of the Legislative Union; they were shot down in the interests of Irish capitalists. Hence, when a Sinn Feiner waxes eloquent about restoring the Constitution of '82, but remains silent about the increasing industrial despotism of the capitalist; when the

Sinn Feiner speaks to men who are fighting against low wages and tells them that the Sinn Fein body has promised lots of Irish labour at low wages to any foreign capitalist who wishes to establish in Ireland, what wonder if they come to believe that a change from Toryism to Sinn Feinism would simply be a change from the devil they do know to the devil they do not know!

The other section of Socialists in Ireland are those who inscribe their banners with the watchword 'Irish Socialist Republic,' who teach that Socialism will mean in Ireland the common ownership by Irish people of the land and everything else necessary to feed, clothe, house and maintain life in Ireland and that therefore Socialism in its application to Ireland means and requires the fullest trust of the Irish people as the arbiters of their own destinies in conformity with the laws of progress and humanity.

This section of Socialists were so Irish that they organised and led the great anti-Jubilee procession of 1897 in Dublin, which completely destroyed all the carefully-prepared British preparations to represent Irish as loyal; and yet their position was so correct from their standpoint that at the International Congress of 1900 at Paris they were granted, in the name of Ireland, separate representation from England and treated and acted as a separate nation.

Now the problem is to find a basis of union on which all these sections who owe allegiance to one or other conception Socialism may unite. My position is that this union, or rapprochement, cannot be arrived at by discussing our differences. Let us rather find out and unite upon the things upon which we agree. Once we get together, we will find that our differences are not so insuperable as they appear whilst we are separated. What is necessary first is a simple platform around which to gather, with the understanding that as much as possible shall be left to future conditions to dictate and as little as possible settled now by rules or theories. As each section has complete confidence in their own doctrines, let them show their confidence by entering an organisation with those who differ from them in methods, and depend upon the development of events to prove the correctness of their position. Each person to have complete freedom of speech in conformity with the common object; the lecture platform to be common to all, and every lecture to be followed by questions and discussion. With mutual toleration on both sides, the Protestant worker may learn that the co-operation of the Catholic who works, suffers, votes and fights alongside him is more immediately vital to his cause and victory day by day than the co-operation of workers on the other side of the Channel; and that Socialists outside of Ireland are all in favour of that national independence which he rejects for the sake of a few worthless votes.

And the Catholic Sinn Feiners may learn that love of freedom beats strongly in the breasts of Protestant peasants and workmen who, because they have approached it from a different historical standpoint, regard the Nationalist conception with suspicion or even hostility.

Ballots, Bullets, Or —

(October, 1909)

Not the least of the services our comrade, Victor Berger, has rendered to the socialist cause must be accounted the writing and publishing of that now famous article in which he draws the attention of his readers to the possibility that the ballot will yet be stricken from the hands of the socialist party, and raises the question of the action our party must take in such an emergency.

It must be confessed, however, that the question has not been faced at all squarely by the majority of the critics who have unburdened themselves upon the matter. We have had much astonishment expressed, a great deal of deprecation of the introduction of the question at the present time, and not a little sly fun poked at our comrade. But one would have thought that a question of such a character brought up for discussion by a comrade noted for his moderation - a moderation by some thought to be akin to compromise - would have induced in socialists a desire to seriously consider the elements of fact and probability behind and inspiring the question. What are these facts?

Briefly stated, the facts as they are known to us all are that all over the United States the capitalist class is even now busily devising ways and means by which the working class can be disfranchised. In

California it is being done by exacting an enormous sum for the right to place a ticket upon the ballot; in Minnesota the same end is sought by a new primary law; in the south by an educational (?) test to be imposed only upon those who possess no property; in some States by imposing a property qualification upon candidates; and all over by wholesale counting out of socialist ballots, and wholesale counting in of fraudulent votes. In addition to this we have had in Colorado and elsewhere many cases where the hired thugs of the capitalists forcibly occupied the polling booths, drove away the real voters and themselves voted in the name of every citizen on the list.

These are a few of the facts. Now what are the probabilities? One is that the capitalist class will not wait until we get a majority at the ballot box, but will precipitate a fight upon some fake issue whilst the mass of the workers are still undecided as to the claims of capitalism and socialism.

Another is that even if the capitalist class were law-abiding enough, or had miscalculated public opinion enough, to wait until the socialists had got a majority at the ballot box in some presidential election, they would then refuse to vacate their offices, or to recognise the election, and with the Senate and the military in their hands would calmly proceed to seat those candidates for President, etc., who had received the highest votes from the capitalistic electorate. As to the first of these probabilities, the issue upon which a socialist success at the ballot box can be averted from the capitalist class is already here, and I expect at any time to see it quietly but effectually materialise. It is this: we have often seen the capitalist class invoke the aid of the Supreme Court in order to save it some petty annoyance by declaring unconstitutional some so-called labour or other legislation. Now I can conceive of no reason why this same Supreme Court cannot be invoked to declare unconstitutional any or all electoral victories of the socialist party. Some may consider this farfetched. I do not consider it nearly as far-fetched as the decision which applied the antitrust laws solely to trade unions, or used the Inter-State Commerce Acts to prevent strikes upon railways.

I consider that if the capitalist class appealed to the Supreme Court and interrogated it to declare whether a political party which aimed at overthrowing the constitution of the United States could legally operate to that end within the constitution of the United States the answer in the negative which that Court would undoubtedly give would not only be entirely logical, but would also be extremely likely to satisfy every shallow thinker and fanatical ancestor-worshipper in the country.

And if such an eventuality arose, and the ballot was, in comrade Berger's words, stricken out of our hands, it would be too late then to propound the query which our comrade propounds now, and ask our friends and supporters: what are you going to do about it?

But even while admitting, nay, urging all this on behalf of the pertinency of our comrade's query, it does not follow that I therefore endorse or recommend his alternative. The rifle is, of course, a useful weapon under certain circumstances, but these circumstances are little likely to occur. This is an age of complicated machinery in war as in industry, and confronted with machine guns, and artillery which kill at seven miles distance, rifles are not likely to be of much material value in assisting in the solution of the labour question in a proletarian manner. It would do comrade Berger good to read a little of the conquests of his countryman, Count Zeppelin, over the domain of the air, and thus think of the futility of opposing even an armed working class to such a power as the airship. Americans have been so enamoured of the achievements of the Wright brothers that too little attention has been paid to the development of the balloon by Zeppelin. Yet in his hands it has evolved into the most perfect and formidable fighting machine ever dreamt of. The words 'dirigible balloon' seem scarcely applicable to his creation. It is a balloon, and more. It is a floating ship, divided into a large number of separate compartments, so that the piercing of one even by a shell leaves the others intact and the machine still floating. Nothing less than fire can menace it with immediate destruction. It can carry seventeen tons and with that weight on board can be guided at will, perform all sorts of figures and evolutions, rise or descend, travel fast or remain stationary. It has already been equipped with a quick-firing Krupp gun and shells made for its own special use, and at the tests of the German army has proven itself capable of keeping up a rapid and sustained fire without interfering with its floating or manoeuvring powers. No army on earth, even of highly trained and disciplined men, could withstand an attack from ten of those monsters for as many minutes. It is more than probable that the development of these machines will eventuate in an armed truce from military conquest by the international capitalist class, the consecration of the flying machine to the cold task of holding in check the working class, and the making safe and profitable all sorts of attacks upon social and political rights. In facing such a weapon in the hands of our remorseless and unscrupulous masters the gun of comrade Victor Berger will be as ineffective as the paper ballot in the hands of a reformer.

Is the outlook, then, hopeless? No! We still have the opportunity to forge a weapon capable of winning the fight for us against political usurpation and all the military powers of earth, sea or air. That weapon is to be forged in the furnace of the struggle in the workshop, mine, factory or railroad, and its name is industrial unionism.

A working class organised on the lines on which the capitalist class has built its industrial plants today, regarding every such plant as the true unit of organisation and society as a whole as the sum total of those units, and ever patiently indoctrinated with the idea that the mission of unionism is to take hold of the industrial equipment of society, and erect itself into the real holding and administrative force of the world; such a revolutionary working class would have a power at its command greater than all the achievements of science can put in the hands of the master class. An injunction forbidding the workers of an industrial union to do a certain thing in the interest of labour would be followed by every member of the union doing that thing until jails became eagerly sought as places of honour, and the fact of having been in one would be as proudly vaunted as is now service on the field of Gettysburg; a Supreme Court decision declaring invalid a socialist victory in a certain district could be met by a general strike of all the workers in that district, supported by the organisation all over the country, and by a relentless boycott extending into the private life of all who supported the fraudulently elected officials. Such a union would revive and apply to the class war of the workers the methods and principles so successfully applied by the peasants of Germany in the Vehmgericht, and by those of the Land League in the land war in Ireland in the eighties.

And eventually, in case of a Supreme Court decision rendering illegal the political activities of the socialist party, or instructing the capitalist officials to refuse to vacate their offices after a national victory by that party, the industrially organised workers would give the usurping government a Roland for its Oliver by refusing to recognise its officers, to transport or feed its troops, to transmit its messages, to print its notices, or to chronicle its doings by working in any newspaper which upheld it. Finally, after having thus demonstrated the helplessness of capitalist officialdom in the face of united action by the producers (by attacking said officialdom with economic paralysis instead of rifle bullets) the industrially organised working class could proceed to take possession of the industries of the country after informing the military and other coercive forces of capitalism that they could procure the necessaries of life by surrendering themselves to the lawfully elected government and renouncing the usurpers at Washington. Otherwise they would have to try and feed and maintain themselves. In the face of such organisation the airships would be as helpless as pirates without a port of call, and military power a broken reed.

The discipline of the military forces before which comrade Berger's rifles would break like glass would dissolve, and the authority of officers would be non-effectual if the soldiery were required to turn into uniformed banditti scouring the country for provisions.

Ireland during the Land League, Paris during the strike of the postmen and telegraphers, the south of France during the strike of the wine growers, the strike of the peasants at Parma, Italy, all were miniature demonstrations of the effectiveness of this method of warfare, all were so many rehearsals in part for this great drama of social revolution, all were object lessons teaching the workers how to extract the virtue from the guns of the political masters.

Erin's Hope: The End & The Means
(1909)

"Our Independence must be had at all hazards. If the men of property will not help us, they must fall; we will free ourselves by the aid of that large and respectable class of the community – the men of no property."

– Theobald Wolfe Tone

Introduction

In publishing an American edition of *Erin's Hope* in the interest of the Irish Socialist Federation, the author is of opinion that a few words of explanation of the circumstances attending its first publication in Ireland in 1897 may be both useful and interesting.

The Irish Socialist Republican Party was founded in Dublin in 1896 by a few workingmen whom the author had succeeded in interesting in his proposition that the two currents of revolutionary thought in Ireland – the Socialist and the National – were not antagonistic, but complementary, and that the Irish Socialist was in reality the best Irish patriot, but that in order to convince the Irish people of that fact he must first of all learn to look inward upon Ireland for his justification, rest his arguments upon the facts of Irish history, and be the champion against the subjection of Ireland and all that it implies. That the Irish National question was at bottom an economic question, and that the economic struggle must first be able to function freely nationally before it could function internationally, and as Socialists were opposed to all oppression, so they should ever be foremost in the daily battle against all its manifestations, social and political. As the embodiment of this teaching, the party adopted the watchword, Irish Socialist Republic, and by deduction therefrom, the aforementioned name of their organization.

This policy received its formal endorsement by the International Socialist movement when at the International Socialist Congress at Paris in 1900 the delegates of the I.S.R.P. were formally seated as the delegates of a nation separate from England.

It is no exaggeration to say that this organization and its policy completely revolutionized advanced politics in Ireland. When it was first initiated the word 'republic' was looked upon as a word to be only whispered among intimates; the Socialists boldly advised the driving from public life of all who would not openly accept it. The thought of revolution was the exclusive possession of a few remnants of the secret societies of a past generation, and was never mentioned by them except with heads closely together and eyes fearfully glancing around; the Socialists broke through this ridiculous secrecy, and in hundreds of speeches in the most public places of the metropolis, as well as in scores of thousands of pieces of literature scattered through the country, announced their purpose to muster all the forces of labor for a revolutionary reconstruction of society and the incidental destruction of the British Empire. The Socialists of Dublin conceived of and organized the great Anti-Jubilee Protest of 1897, which startled the world and shattered all the elaborate attempts of the British government to represent Ireland as loyal. They held the first meeting of protest against the Boer war, and at that meeting of over 2,000 persons in College Green, Dublin, passed the first resolution in Ireland calling upon the Irish in the Transvaal to take up arms against the armies of the British capitalist government; they conducted the first campaign against enlistment in the army; they were the first to contest elections upon a platform openly declaring for a revolution, and they were the first to point out all the immense amelioration of the conditions of life in Ireland which could be realized without waiting for Home Rule. In short, the Irish Socialist Republican Party has to itself the credit of having opened up practically all the new fields of thought and action now being exploited by other and less revolutionary organizations.

Needless to say, when this policy was first entered upon it aroused interest alike among Nationalists and Socialists. Thence came requests for enlightenment, each side inquiring upon that part of the policy which seemed to touch most closely their own previous ideas of politics. The advanced nationalists of Ireland had at that time only one monthly literary magazine, the *Shan Van Vocht*, ably edited by Miss Alice Milligan and published at Belfast. In response to a request from that lady, the article, "Can Irish Republicans be Politicians?" was written and published in that magazine in November, 1896. Mr. J. Keir Hardie, the editor of the *Labor Leader,* Glasgow, and Socialist member of the English Parliament, also wrote asking for a series of articles upon the relation of the Irish question to Socialism, and in response to the invitation, the other articles were written. The I.S.R.P. afterwards combined the two sets of articles and made of them the pamphlet which we now reproduce.

We now present those articles to the Irish Workers in America in hope that we may induce them to study and accept our position, viz.:

That the Irish question is at bottom a Social question, that Socialism alone can lay the material foundation necessary for the free development of the intellectual and spiritual forces of the scattered children of the Clan-na-Gael, and that the Socialist message to Ireland and to America is identical, and calls for the Industrial and Political Organization of Labor as the Means by which that End may be reached.

Erin's Hope

In the October issue of the *Shan Van Vocht*, the editor, in commenting upon the strictures passed by one contributor on the French Revolution, asks for an expression of opinion on the relative merits of revolutionary uprisings and moral force agitations. As both the article in question and the editorial note suggesting the discussion, apparently take it for granted that the query with which this communication is headed, must be answered in the negative, an assumption which I believe to be entirely erroneous, and the fundamental mistake in the calculation of our modern Irish revolutionists, I would suggest that as the broader and more comprehensive question, this be instead the basis of the proposed controversy. To make my position more plain, I may say, I write as one who believes that the concession to Ireland of such a limited form of local autonomy as that embodied in Mr. Gladstone's Home Rule Bill, would not, in any sense, be a step towards independence, but would more likely create effectual barriers in the way of its realization.

The question thus arises, are those who see in an Irish Republic the only political ideal worth striving for to eschew political action and seek, in secret conspiracy alone, to prepare for revolution? Up to the present every genuine Irish revolutionist has acted on this belief, that political action was impossible for republicans.

Now I assert the contrary. A revolution can only succeed in any country when it has the moral sanction of the people. It is so, even in an independent country; it is doubly so in a country subject like Ireland, to the rule of another. Within this century, no Irish revolutionist had obtained this sanction before he took the field. In 1848 the majority of the Irish people pinned their faith to the Repeal Association, which had disavowed even the right to resist oppression, and the Young Irelanders themselves had made no reasonable effort to prepare the popular mind for revolution, but had rather been precipitated into it against their will. Under such conditions, failure was inevitable. Those who were willing to 'rise' had no means of knowing how far their aspirations were shared by their fellow-countrymen elsewhere, and lacking confidence in themselves, with the recognized leaders of public opinion against them, the effort ended in disaster. The history of the Fenian movement was somewhat similar. The number of actually enrolled members formed but an insignificant minority of the population, the vast majority of our countrymen, though perhaps sympathizing with the Fenian ideal, put their trust in politicians who preached tame submission under the name of 'prudence' and 'caution,' and in the critical period of the movement flung the weight of their influence on the side of 'law and order.'

In both cases the recognized leaders of national thought were on the side of constituted authority, and against every revolutionary effort. The facts are as undeniable as they are lamentable, and they speak in trumpet tones in favor of such a re-modelling of Irish revolutionary tactics as shall prevent a recurrence of similar disasters in the future. This, I hold, can be best accomplished by a political party seeking to give public expression to the republican ideal. One point needs to be emphasized in this connection, viz., it is not republicanism, but the counsel of insurrectionary effort to realize republicanism, which gave to previous Irish movements their odor of illegality. A candidate for political honors (?) is as much at liberty to put the attainment of a republic on his programme as he is to pledge himself to Home Rule, or any other scheme of political reconstruction. Were a political party formed in Ireland to educate the people in sound national ideas by pledging every candidate to openly repudiate the authority of the Crown, and work for the realization of republican principles, it would achieve a much needed transformation in Irish politics.

Hitherto every Irish agitation has sought to make its programme as broad and loosely defined as possible, in order to enrol under its banner every section of Irish national opinion – loyal Home Rulers, Conservative Nationalists, Compromising Whigs, and Nationalist Democrats – all alike were welcome. Such a basis is undoubtedly best for the purposes of an 'agitation', but it is worse than useless for the purposes of earnest revolutionists seeking a definite end. But such a party as I speak of, with an avowedly republican programme, would, in its very definiteness and coherence, have immense advantage to recommend it to the consideration and support of practical-minded men. It would prevent the emasculation of our young men by the vaporings of 'constitutional' patriots; it would effectually expose the sham Nationalists, and, let us hope, drive them from political life; it would at every election in which it took part, afford a plebiscite of the people for or against the republic; it would enlist the sympathy of many earnest patriots whose open natures shrink from secret conspiracy; it would ascertain with mathematical accuracy the moment when the majority of the Irish people were ripe for revolution, and it could not be suppressed while representative government was left in Ireland.

By adhering steadily to the policy of pledging every candidate to its full programme, whether they stood for Parliament or local governing bodies, it would insure that when a majority of the Irish people had at the ballot boxes declared in favor of the revolutionary party every soldier of the cause would know that in the fight he was waging, he was not merely one of a numerically insignificant band of malcontents, but a citizen soldier fighting under orders publicly expressed in face of all the world by a majority of his fellow-countrymen. This, I hold to be an eminently practical method of obtaining our end. It would exclude the possibility of our national principles being betrayed in the moment of danger, or compromised in the hour of success to suit the convenience of interested party politicians; it would inspire confidence in the most timid by its recognition of the fact that to counsel rebellion without first obtaining the moral sanction of the people would be an act of criminal folly which would only end in disaster. It would make Irish republicanism no longer the 'politics of despair', but the Science of Revolution.

It may be urged against such a proposal that the first need of Irish politics is unity, and that such a party would only accentuate the division at present existing. This, however, could only be the case if our present representatives refuse to accept the pledge of loyalty to the free Irish Republic, and to it alone. If they do so refuse, then they are unfit to be representatives of the Irish democracy, and cannot be removed too soon. The objection in itself implies a suspicion of the genuine nature of the patriotism so loudly vaunted by our party politicians. Unity is a good thing, no doubt, but honesty is better, and if unity can only be obtained by the suppression of truth and the toleration of falsehood, then it is not worth the price we are asked to pay for it. I would, in conclusion, earnestly recommend my readers to study the suggestions contained in this paper, and to act accordingly. Should this meet with a favorable reception, I may give in a future issue my ideas on the programme of political and social reform, on which such a party might fight in Parliament and the country, while the public opinion of Ireland was ripening behind them, and pending the arrival of the propitious moment for action.

Ireland before the Conquest

"Before the time of the conquest, the Irish people knew nothing of absolute property in land. The land belonged to the entire sept; the chief was little more than managing member of the association. The feudal idea which came in with the conquest was associated with foreign dominion, and has never to this day been recognized by the moral sentiment of the people."

In these few words of Mr. John Stuart Mill the impartial student may find the key for unravelling the whole tangled skein of Irish politics. Latter-day politicians, both on the English and Irish side, have done their utmost to familiarize the public mind with the belief that the Irish question arises solely out of the aspirations of the Irish people to have more complete control over the internal administration of the affairs of their country than it is possible for them to exercise while the seat of goverment is located at Westminster, and that, therefore, some form of local self-government, as, for instance, Mr. Gladstone's Home Rule Bill, is all that is needed to settle this question, and lay forever the troubled spirit of Irish discontent. According to this luminous (?) exposition of Irish history, we are to believe that the two nations have for seven hundred years been engaged in unceasing warfare, that the one country (Ireland) has during all that time been compelled to witness the merciless slaughter of her children by famine, pestilence and the sword; that each succeeding generation has witnessed a renewal of the conflict and a renewal of the martyrdom, until the sensitive mind recoils from a perusal of Irish history as from the records of a shambles, and all, forsooth, because Irishmen and Englishmen could not agree upon the form of political administration best suited for Ireland.

If this new reading of Irish history were true the intelligent foreigner might be forgiven for rating at a very low standard the intelligence of the two nations which during seven hundred years had not evolved a satisfactory solution of such a simple question. At precisely the same low standard may safely be rated the political acumen of the English and Irish party leaders who are today complacently trotting out the discredited abortion of Home Rule as a sovereign remedy for Ireland's misery.

The Irish question has, in fact, a much deeper source than a mere difference of opinion on forms of government. Its real origin and inner meaning lay in the circumstances that the two opposing nations held fundamentally different ideas upon the vital question of property in land. Recent scientific research by such eminent sociologists as Letourneau, Lewis Morgan, Sir Henry Maine, and others has amply demonstrated the fact that common ownership of land formed the basis of primitive society in almost every country. But whereas in the majority of countries now called civilized such primitive communion had almost entirely disappeared before the dawn of history, and had at no time acquired a higher status than that conferred by the social sanction of unlettered and uneducated tribes, in Ireland the system formed part of the well-defined social organization of a nation of scholars and students, recognized by Chief and Tanist, Brehon and Bard, as the inspiring principle of their collective life, and the basis of their national system of jurisprudence. Such a striking fact will, of course, be interpreted in many ways, according to the temperament and political or racial sympathies of the reader. The adherent of the present order of society will regard it as proof of the Irish incapacity for assimilating progressive ideas, and will, no doubt, confidently assert that this incapacity is the real source of Ireland's misery, since it has unfitted her sons for the competitive scramble for existence, and so fore-doomed them to the lot of hewers of wood and drawers of water.

The ardent student of sociology, who believes that the progress of the human race through the various economic stages of communism, chattel slavery, feudalism, and wage-slavery, has been but a preparation for the higher ordered society of the future; that the most industrially advanced countries are but, albeit often unconsciously, developing the social conditions which, since the breakup of universal tribal communism, have been rendered historically necessary for the inauguration of a new and juster economic order, in which social, political and national antagonism will be unknown, will perhaps regard the Irish adherence to clan ownership at such a comparatively recent date as the Seventeenth Century as an evidence of retarded economical development, and therefore a real hindrance to progress. But the sympathetic student of history, who believes in the possibility of a people by political intuition anticipating the lessons afterwards revealed to them in the sad school of experience, will not be indisposed to join with the ardent Irish patriot in his lavish expressions of admiration for the sagacity of his Celtic forefathers, who foreshadowed in the democratic organization of the Irish clan the more perfect organization of the free society of the future.

Whichever be the true interpretation of Irish history, one fact at least stands out clear and undeniable, viz., that the conflict between the rival systems of land ownership was the pivot around which centered all the struggles and rebellions of which that history has been so prolific. The Irish regarded with inveterate hostility their English rulers, at all times set little store upon promises of incorporation within the pale of the constitution, and rose with enthusiasm under their respective rebel chiefs, because they regarded this as the all-important question, because in their eyes English rule and Dublin parliaments were alike identified as the introducers and upholders of the system of feudalism and private ownership of land, as opposed to the Celtic system of clan or common ownership, which they regarded, and, I think, rightly, as the pledge at once of their political and social liberty.

The English Government were also astute enough to perceive that the political or national subjection of Ireland was entirely valueless to the conquerors while the politically subjected nation remained in possession of economic freedom. Consequently, we find that the first stipulation made to the Irish tribe upon its submission always provided that the lands of the tribe should be regarded as the private property of the chief; that he should therefore accept them as a grant from the crown, from which he should in future hold them; that he should drop his Irish title, which proclaimed him the freely elected chief of a free community, and should instead accept an English title, such as duke or earl, and in all things conform to English ideas of civilization and social order. All these stipulations were in the last degree repugnant to Irish ideas. The chief, as Mill has justly observed, was but the managing member of the tribal association, although in the stress of constant warfare they usually limited their choice to the members of one or two families; yet the right of election was never abdicated by the tribesmen. Whenever the seductions of English gold overmastered the patriotism of an Irish chief and succeeded in inducing his acceptance of the alien property system and the alien title (as in the case of Art O'Neil and Nial Garbh O'Donnell, the Queen's O'Reilly and the Queen's Maguire), they immediately elected another chief in his stead; and from that moment the unfortunate renegade became an outlaw from his own people, and could only appear in his native territory under an escort of English Spears.

The Irish System was thus on a par with those conceptions of social rights and duties which we find the ruling classes today denouncing so fiercely as 'Socialistic'. It was apparently inspired by the democratic principle that property was intended to serve the people, and not by the principle so universally acted upon at present, viz., that the people have no other function in existing than to be the bondslaves of those who by force or by fraud have managed to possess themselves of property. They did not, indeed, regard all forms of productive property as rightfully belonging to the community; but when we remember that the land alone was at that time of importance, all other forms of property being insignificant by comparison, we see that they were as Socialistic as the industrial development of their time required. The English civilization against which they fought was, on the other hand, thoroughly individualistic; and, as it triumphed, we are reaping the fruits to-day in the industrial disputes, the agricultural depressions, the poorhouses, and other such glorious institutions in Church and State as we are permitted the luxury of enjoying in common with our fellow-subjects in this 'integral portion of the British Empire'. The results of the change on the national life of Erin are well illustrated in the scornful words in which Aubrey De Vere apostrophizes the new race of exploiters which then arose:

"The chiefs of the Gael were the people embodied; The chiefs were the blossoms, the people the root. Their conquerors, the Normans, high-souled and high-blooded, Grew Irish at last from the scalp to the foot; And ye, ye are hirelings and satraps, not nobles – Your slaves they detest you, your masters, they scorn; The river lives on, but the sun-painted bubbles Pass quickly, to the rapids incessantly borne."

Ireland under British rule

The break-up of the Kilkenny Confederation in 1649, and the consequent dispersion of the Irish clans, was the immediate cause of that confusion of thought and apparent lack of directness in aim which down to our day has characterized all modern Irish politics. Deprived of any form of political or social organization which might serve as an effective basis for its practical realization, the demand for the common ownership of the land naturally fell into abeyance until such time as the conquest of some form of political freedom should enable the dispossessed Irishry to substitute for the lost tribal association the fuller and broader conception of an Irish nation as the natural repository and guardian of the people's heritage. But when the fusing process of a common subjection had once more welded the heterogenous elements of Irish society into one compact nationality it was found that in the intervening period a new class had arisen in the land – a class which, while professedly ultra-nationalistic in its political aims, had nevertheless so far compounded with the enemy as to accept the alien social system, with its accompanying manifestations, the legal dispossession and economic dependence of the vast mass of the Irish people, as part of the natural order of society.

The Irish middle class, who then by virtue of their social position and education stepped to the front as Irish patriot leaders, owed their unique status in political life to two entirely distinct and apparently antagonistic causes. Their wealth they derived from the manner in which they had contrived to wedge themselves into a place in the commercial life of the 'Saxon enemy', assimilating his ideas and adopting his methods, until they often proved the most ruthless of the two races in pushing to its furthest limits their powers of exploitation. Their political influence they derived from their readiness at all times to do lip service to the cause of Irish nationality, which in their phraseology meant simply the transfer of the seat of government from London to Dublin, and the consequent transfer to their own or their relatives' pockets of some portion of the legislative fees and lawyers pickings then, as at present, expended among the Cockneys. With such men at the helm it is no wonder that the patriot parties of Ireland have always ended their journey upon the rock of disaster. Beginning by accepting a social system abhorrent to the best traditions of a Celtic people, they next abandoned as impossible the realization of national independence. By the first act they set the seal of their approval upon a system founded upon the robbery of their countrymen, and by the second they bound up the destinies of their country with the fate of an Empire in the humiliation of whose piratical rulers lies the Irish people's only chance of national and social redemption.

As compensation for this gross betrayal the middle class politicians offer – Home Rule. To exactly analyse what Home Rule would confer on Ireland is a somewhat difficult task, since every one interprets the 'thing' in his own way and according to his own peculiar bent. Perhaps the safest way, and at any rate the one least open to objection, will be to regard as Home Rule the Bill introduced by Mr. Gladstone. As this scheme represents the utmost that the statesmanlike prowess of Mr. Parnell, with a solid phalanx of eighty-six members behind him, could wrest from the fear or favor of English Liberalism, it is surely safe enough to assume that no other merely political body from Ireland is ever likely to improve upon this concession by any alliance with either of the great factions who watch over the interests of the English propertied class. Home Rule proposed to establish in Ireland a domestic legislature that would be carefully divested of all those powers and attributes which by the common consent of civilized peoples are regarded as properly belonging to the sphere and functions of government; that would have no power in controlling diplomacy, post office, commerce, telegraphs, coinage, customs and excise, weights and measures, copyrights and patents, succession to the Crown, or army, navy, militia or volunteers.

The only conceivable result of such a state of affairs would have been to create in Ireland a host of place-hunters and Government officials, who, secure in the enjoyment of a good income themselves, would have always acted as a barrier between the people and their oppressors. As a method whereby the English legislature might have been relieved of some of its duties at home, and thus left more free to pursue its policy of plunder and aggression abroad, it ought to have delighted the heart of the Jingo politicians. That they were too dunderheaded to see their opportunity is a mercy for which far-seeing Irish democrats can never be sufficiently thankful.

The second Home Rule Bill was slightly more democratic than the first, therefore the Government made no effort to force it upon the Upper House. The English Liberal Party – the most treacherous political party in Europe – has always had two favorite devices for destroying obnoxious proposals of reform. First: unscrupulous slander and opposition; second: theoretical acceptance of the principle of reform, but indefinite postponement of its practical realization, continued on one pretext or another, until the hearts of the reformers are broken and their organizations disrupted. The first was defeated by the genius of Parnell; how well the second method has succeeded let the present political chaos of Ireland testify.

Realising that taken on its own merits, Home Rule is simply a mockery of Irish national aspirations, our middle class leaders have industriously instilled into the public mind the belief that the advent of Home Rule would mean the immediate establishment of manufactures and the opening up of mines, etc., in every part of Ireland. This seems to them the highest possible ideal – an Irish society composed of employers making fortunes and workers grinding out their lives for a weekly wage. But, to say the least, the men who talk in this manner must either be woefully ignorant of the conditions of modern industry, or else, for some private reason of their own, are wilfully deceiving those who believe in them. To establish industry successfully to-day in any country requires at least two things, neither of which Ireland possesses, and one of which she never can possess. The first is the possession of the wherewithal to purchase machinery and raw materials for the equipment of her factories, and the second is customers to purchase the goods when they are manufactured. Now, we find that England, who has had the start in manufacturing over every other nation, who has been extending her commerce and perfecting her machinery for a hundred and fifty years at least, who has created a nation of highly skilled artisans, adept in every form of industrial achievement – England, the wealthiest country in the world, has brought her industries to such a degree of mechanical perfection that her customers cannot keep her going. She can supply goods of every description much quicker than the world is able to purchase and consume them, and as a direct consequence of this vast producing power she is compelled every few years to either wholly or partially stop her machinery and close her factories, to discharge her artisan subjects, and compel them to walk about in enforced idleness and semi-starvation until such time as the goods they have produced are purchased and consumed by other people – their customers.

Bear this in mind, and remember also, that Germany, France, Italy, Belgium, Austria, Russia, every state on the continent of Europe and America, India, China and Japan, are all entering into the struggle; that each of them is striving hard, not only to provide what it had formerly relied on England to provide, but also to beat England out of the markets of the world. Remember that for all those countries the great difficulty is to find customers, that the old-established firm in the business – viz., the British Empire – finds that her customers cannot keep her mills and factories going. Remember all this, and then tell me how poor Ireland, exhausted and drained of her life-blood at every pore, with a population almost wholly agricultural and unused to mechanical pursuits, is to establish new factories, and where she is to find the customers to keep them going. She cannot create new markets. This world is only limited after all, and the nations of Europe are pushing their way into its remote corners so rapidly that in a few years time, at most, the entire world will have been exhausted as a market for their wares.

Go to the factory towns, to the ship-building centers, to the coal mines, to the Trade Unions, or to the Stock Exchanges of England, the continent of Europe or America, and everywhere you will hear the same cry: "The supply of cotton and linen goods, of ironwork, of coal and of ships of every description, is exceeding the demand; we must work short time, we must reduce the workers' wages, we must close our factories – there is not enough customers to keep our machinery going." In the face of such facts the thoughtful Irish patriot will throw rant aside and freely recognize that it is impossible for Ireland to do what those other countries cannot do, with their greater advantages, viz., to attain prosperity by establishing a manufacturing system in a world-market already glutted with every conceivable kind of commodity. It is well also to remember that even under the most favorable circumstances, even if by some miracle, we were able to cover the green fields of Erin with huge, ugly factories, with chimneys belching forth volumes of poisonous smoke and coating the island with a sooty desolation – even then we would quickly find that under the conditions born of the capitalist system our one hope of keeping our feet as a manufacturing nation would depend upon our ability to work longer and harder for a lower wage than the other nations of Europe, in order that our middle class may have the opportunity of selling their goods at a lower price than their competitors. This is equivalent to saying that our chance of making Ireland a manufacturing country depends upon us becoming the lowest blacklegs in Europe. Even then the efforts would be doomed to failure, for the advent of the yellow man into the competitive arena, the sudden development of the capitalist system on China and Japan, has rendered forever impossible the uprise of another industrial nation in Europe.

Again, it is said we need not perhaps establish industry or try it, but we can at least establish peasant proprietary, and make every man the owner of his farm, let every man live, if not under his own vine and fig tree, at least upon his own potato patch. In the first place, I consider such an act to be, even if practicable, one of very questionable justice. To make the land of a country the property of a class is to my mind equally iniquitous, whether that class number a few hundreds or a few thousands. The land of a country belongs of right to the people of that country, and not to any particular class, nor even to any single generation of the people. The private ownership of land by the landlord class is an injustice to the whole community, but the creation of a peasant proprietary would only tend to stereotype and consecrate that injustice, since it would leave out of account the entire laboring class as well as the dispossessed millions of former tenants whom landlord rule had driven into the Irish towns or across the sea.

It is, of course, manifestly impossible to reinstate the Irish people on the lands from which they have been driven, but that fact only lends additional point to the demand for the nationalization of land in the hands of the Irish State. Setting that fact aside, however, have our advocates of peasant proprietary really considered the economic tendencies of the time, and the development of the mechanical arts in the agricultural world. The world is progressive, and peasant proprietary, which a hundred years ago might have been a boon, would now be powerless to save from ruin the agriculture of Ireland. The day of small farmers, as of small capitalists, is gone, and wherever they are still found they find it impossible to compete with the improved machinery and mammoth farms of America and Australia. Whereas each Irish farm is burdened with the support of its field workers for the entire 365 days in the year, the capitalist farmer of the States hires his 'hands' by the hundred for harvesting operations, and discharges them immediately it is completed, thus reducing to one-fourth the annual wages bill of his workers.

How are our small farmers to compete with a state of matters like this, or like unto that revealed in the report of the American Social Science Association, even as far back as 1878? It tells how science and invention, after devoting so much time to industry, have turned their attention to agriculture, and as a result have effected almost a revolution in that branch of human activity. Ploughs which, driven by horses, plough more than five acres per day, or the extent of many an Irish farm, and steam ploughs which do much more; machines for sowing seeds, with which a boy and horse can do three times the work of a man, and do it much better; reaping machines, with which a man with one or two pairs of horses can do the work of at least sixty men with reaping hooks; reaping machines which not only cut the harvest, but tie it as well, are now so common in England and America as to fail to attract attention, and we hear on good authority of machines which cut, thrash, winnow, and sack it, without the intervention of any other human hands than those of the engineer who tends the machine. In cutting the corn a man or boy, with a horse and machine, can do the work of twenty men cutting an acre an hour.

All this, be it remembered, is only possible to the farmer who holds his thousands of acres. The first cost of any one of those machines would be enough to ruin the average small farmer in Ireland, and the result is that while he is painfully laboring on his farm his American competitor can bring in his harvest, send it thousands of miles by railroad, load it into ships, send it across the Atlantic, and eventually sell it practically at our doors as cheap as, and cheaper than, our home produce. The competition of New Zealand beef and frozen mutton has already inflicted incalculable harm upon the Irish cattle trade, and within the last few months I have received private information of a contract entered into with the Peninsular and Oriental Steamship Company to transport butter from the huge cattle ranches of Australia to any port in Great Britain and Ireland at a price that spells ruin to the dairy farms of these countries. While, then, in order to avoid even the appearance of injustice, we may rigidly respect those 'rights of property' in land our peasant farmers have acquired by purchase, we must recognize that peasant proprietary in itself offers no hope of a free and unanxious life – not even to the peasant proprietor.

Ireland's future

Ere we can forecast the future we must understand the present and bring a just sense of proportion to our review of the history of the past. What, then, are the conditions which govern life in Ireland today, and of what are those conditions the outcome? According to the most eminent authorities who have ever dealt with the subject the soil of Ireland is capable of sustaining a population many times larger than she has ever borne upon its surface, yet Ireland is in a state of chronic starvation. Every ship that leaves our ports is laden down with harvest for human consumption, while the people whose strong hands have reaped that harvest pine in wretchedness and want, or fly from the shores of this fertile land as from the arid sands of a desert. The landlord class, infatuated with that madness which always precedes destruction, press for their rents to the uttermost farthing wherever they can wheedle or coerce a too-compliant legislature and executive to support them in their exactions. The capitalist farmer, driven to the wall by the stress of the competition, seeks in vain to maintain his foothold in life by unceasing struggle with the lord of the soil on one hand and a ruthless oppression of the laborer on the other; the small farmer, bereft entirely of hope for the future, settles despairingly into a state of social wretchedness for which no savage land can furnish a parallel; the agricultural laborer, with his fellow in the towns, takes his strength, his brains, his physical and intellectual capabilities to the market, and offers them to his wealthier fellow-creatures, to be exploited in return for a starvation wage. On all sides anarchy and oppression reign supreme, until one could scarcely wonder if even the most orthodox amongst us were tempted to echo the saying of the Spanish Don Juan Aguila after the battle of Kinsale: "Surely Christ never died for this people!"

These are the conditions under which life is endured in Ireland today. From what do such conditions spring? There are two things necessary for the maintenance of life in Ireland, as in every other country. They are land and labor. Possessed of these two essentials, the human race has at its command all the factors requisite for the well-being of the species. From the earth labor extracts alike its foods and the mineral wealth with which it contrives to construct and adorn its habitations and prepare its raiment. Therefore the possession of the soil is everywhere the first requisite of life. Granting this as a proposition too self-evident to need elaborate demonstration, we at once arrive at the conclusion that since the soil is so necessary to our existence the first care of every well-regulated community ought to he to preserve the use of that soil, and the right to freely share in its fruits, to every member of the community, present or prospective, born or unborn.

The moment when the land of a country passes from the care of the community as a public trust, and from being the common property of the entire people becomes the private property of individuals, marks the beginning of slavery for that people and of oppression for that country. With the land held as the property of individuals there are immediately created two antagonistic classes in society – one holding the land and demanding from the other a rent for permission to live upon it, and the other driven by a constant increase of their own numbers to offer larger and larger shares of the produce of their labor as tribute to the first class, who thus become masters of the lives of their fellow-beings. With the land held as the common property of the people an abundant harvest would he eagerly welcomed as an addition to the wealth of the community, guaranteeing against want every one of its members. With the land held as private property the abundant harvest must be sold to satisfy the exactions of the holder of the soil, and as he jingles in his pockets the result of the sale of his tenants' produce the families who reaped it may be perishing of want.

As one crime begets another, so one economic blunder invariably brings in its train a series of blunders, each one more fruitful of disaster than the first. When the production of food for public use was abandoned in favor of production of agricultural produce for private sale and private profit, it was almost inevitable that the production of almost every other necessary of life should be subjected to the same conditions. Thus we find that food, clothes, houses and furniture are not produced in order that people may he fed, clad, sheltered or made comfortable, but rather in order that the class who have obtained possession of the land, machinery, workshops and stores necessary for the production of these essentials should be thereby enabled to make a comfortable living at the expense of their fellow creatures. If the landlord and employing class think they can make a rent or profit by allowing the people to feed, clothe, or house themselves, then the latter are allowed to do so under the direction of the former – when, where, and how the masters please. If, on the contrary, they imagine it will pay them better to refuse that right (as they do in every eviction, strike, or lock-out), then they do refuse that permission, and their countrymen go forth starving, their children die of want before their eyes, and their wives and mothers pine in wretchedness and misery in what their forefathers were wont to call the 'Isle of the Blest'.

By the operation of certain historic causes the workers have been deprived of everything by which they can maintain life and are thus compelled to seek their livelihood by the sale of their capacity for work, their labor power. The worker thus finds that the most essential condition which he must perform in order that he may possess his life is to sell part of that life into the service and for the profit of another. Whether he sells it by the hour, the day, the week, or the month is immaterial – sell it he must or else starve.

Now, the worker is a human being, with all the powers and capabilities of a human being within him, just as is a landlord, a capitalist, or any other ornament of society. But when he approaches the capitalist in order to complete that bargain, which means the sale of his life piecemeal in order that he may enjoy it as a whole, he finds that he must carefully divest himself of all claims to be considered as a human being, and offer himself upon the market subject to the same law as govern the purchase or sale of any inanimate, soulless commodity, such as a pair of boots, a straw hat or a frock coat. That is to say, the price he will receive for this piecemeal sale of himself will depend upon how many more are compelled by hunger to make the same horrible bargain.

In like manner with the farmer seeking to rent a farm in the open market. Each competitor seeks to outbid the other, until the rent is fixed usually out of all proportion to the price which will in the future be obtained for the produce of the farm bidden for. The agriculturist finds that in years of universal plenty, when throughout the world the earth brings forth its fruits in teeming profusion, the excess of supply over effective demand operates to lower the price of his farm produce, until it scarcely repays his labor in garnering it, and in times of scarcity, when a good price might be obtained, he has little to sell, his customers have not the wherewithal to buy, and the landlord or the money lender are as relentless as ever in their exactions.

As a remedy for such an array of evils Home Rule stands revealed as a glaring absurdity. The Home Rule parties either ignore the question altogether or else devote their attention to vain attempts to patch up the system with schemes of reform which each day tends to discredit more and more. The tenant who seeks in the Land Court for a judicial valuation of his holding finds that in face of the steady fall in agricultural prices (assisted by preferential railway rates in favor of foreign produce) the 'fair' rent of one year becomes the rack-rent of another, and the tenant who avails himself of the purchase clauses of the Land Act finds that he has only escaped from the personal tyranny of a landlord to have his veins sucked by the impersonal power of the money lender.

Confronted with such facts, the earnest Irish worker turns in dismay and joins his voice to that of the uncompromising Nationalist in seeking from the advocate of an Irish Socialist Republic the clue of the labyrinthine puzzle of modern economic conditions. The problem is a grave and difficult one, alike from the general ignorance of its controlling conditions and because of the multiplicity of vested interests which must be attacked and overthrown at every forward step towards its solution. The solution herein set forth is therefore not guaranteed to be absolutely perfect in all its details, but only to furnish a rough draft of a scheme of reform by means of which the ground may be prepared for that revolutionary change in the structure of society which can alone establish an approximation to an ideally just social system.

The agriculture of Ireland can no longer compete with the scientifically equipped farmers of America, therefore the only hope that now remains is to abandon competition altogether as a rule of life, to organize agriculture as a public service under the control of boards of management elected by the agricultural population (no longer composed of farmers and laborers, but of free citizens with equal responsibility and equal honor), and responsible to them and the nation at large, and with all the mechanical and scientific aids to agriculture the entire resources of the nation can place at their disposal. Let the produce of Irish soil go first to feed the Irish people, and after a sufficient store has been retained to insure of that being accomplished, let the surplus be exchanged with other countries in return for those manufactured goods Ireland needs but does not herself produce.

Thus we will abolish at one stroke the dread of foreign competition and render perfectly needless any attempt to create an industrial hell in Ireland under the specious pretext of 'developing our resources'.

Apply to manufacture the same social principle, let the co-operative organization of the workers replace the war of classes under capitalism and transform the capitalist himself from an irresponsible hunter after profit into a public servant fulfilling a public function and under public control. Recognize the right of all to an equal opportunity to develop to their fullest capacity all the powers and capabilities inherent in them by guaranteeing to all our countrymen and women, the weak as well as the strong, the simple as well as the cunning, the honest equally with the unscrupulous, the fullest, freest, and most abundant human life intelligently organized society can confer upon any of its members.

"But," you will say, "this means a Socialist Republic; this is subversive of all the institutions upon which the British Empire is founded – this cannot be realized without national independence." Well, I trust no one will accuse me of a desire to fan into flame the dying embers of national hatred when I state as my deliberate and conscientious conviction that the Irish democracy ought to strive consistently after the separation of their country from the yoke that links her destinies with those of the British Crown. The interests of Labor all the world over are identical, it is true, but it is also true that each country had better work out its own salvation on the lines most congenial to its own people.

The national and racial characteristics of the English and Irish people are different, their political history and traditions are antagonistic, the economic development of the one is not on a par with the other, and, finally, although they have been in the closest contact for seven hundred years, yet the Celtic Irishman is to-day as much of an insoluble problem to even the most friendly English as on the day when the two countries were first joined in unholy wedlock. No Irish revoutionist worth his salt would refuse to lend a hand to the Social Democracy of England in the effort to uproot the social system of which the British Empire is the crown and apex, and in like manner no English Social Democrat fails to recognize clearly that the crash which would betoken the fall of the ruling classes in Ireland would sound the tocsin for the revolt of the disinherited in England.

But on whom devolves the task of achieving that downfall of the ruling classes in Ireland? On the Irish people. But who are the Irish people? Is it the dividend-hunting capitalist with the phraseology of patriotism on his lips and the spoil wrung from sweated Irish toilers fill his pockets; is it the scheming lawyer – most immoral of all classes; is it the slum landlord who denounces rackrenting in the country and practices it in the towns; is it any one of these sections who to-day dominate Irish politics? Or is it not rather the Irish working class – the only secure foundation on which a free nation can be reared – the Irish working class which has borne the brunt of every political struggle, and gained by none, and which is to-day the only class in Ireland which has no interest to serve in perpetuating either the political or social forms of oppression – the British connection or the capitalist system? The Irish working class must emancipate itself, and in emancipating itself it must, perforce, free its country. The act of social emancipation requires the conversion of the land and instruments of production from private property into the public or common property of the entire nation. This necessitates a social system of the most absolute democracy, and in establishing that necessary social system the working class must grapple with every form of government which could interfere with the most unfettered control by the people of Ireland of all the resources of their country.

On the Working Class of Ireland, therefore, devolves the task of conquering political representation for their class as the preliminary step towards the conquest of political power. This task can only be safely entered upon by men and women who recognize that the first action of a revolutionary army must harmonize in principle with those likely to be its last, and that, therefore, no revolutionists can safely invite the co-operation of men or classes, whose ideals are not theirs, and whom, therefore, they may be compelled to fight at some future critical stage of the journey to freedom. To this category belongs every section of the propertied class, and every individual of those classes who believes in the righteousness of his class position. The freedom of the working class must be the work of the working class. And let it be remembered that timidity in the slave induces audacity in the tyrant, but the virility and outspokenness of the revolutionists ever frightens the oppressor himself to hide his loathesomeness under the garb of reform. And thus remembering, fight for your class at every point.

Our people are flying to the uttermost ends of the earth; seek to retain them at home by reducing the hours of labor wherever you have the power and by supporting every demand for legislative restriction. Your Irish railways employ thousands of men, whose working hours average twelve per day. Were they restricted to a forty-eight-hour week of labor, employment would be provided for thousands of Irishmen who at present are driven exiles from their native land. Let your representatives demand an eight-hour bill for railways. Our Irish municipalities and other public bodies controlled by popular vote employ also many thousands of men. What are their hours of labor? On the average ten, and their wages just above starvation point. Insist upon Irish corporations establishing the eight-hour day in all their works. They at least do not need to fear foreign competition. If you have no vote in the corporation you can at least help to hound off the political platform elsewhere every so-called patriot who refuses to perform this act of justice. Every Irish corporation which declines to institute an eight-hours' working day at a decent wage for its employees has virtually entered into a conspiracy with the British Government to expatriate the Irish people, rather than pay an additional halfpenny in the pound on the rates. In all our cities the children of the laboring class are dying off before their time for lack of wholesome nourishing food. As our municipalities and public trusts provide water for the people free of direct payment and charge the cost upon the rates, let them also provide at our schools free breakfasts, dinners and teas to the children in attendance there, and pay for it from the same source. No matter what may be the moral character of the parent, let us at least save the helpless children of our race from physical and mental degeneracy, and save our teachers from the impossible task of forcing education upon a child whose brain is enfeebled by the starvation of its body. As the next step in organization, let the corporations and public bodies everywhere throughout the country establish depots for the supply of bread and all the necessaries of life to the people, at cost price and without the intervention of the middleman.

When, in addition to the foregoing reforms, we have demanded the abolition of our hateful poor-house system, and the imposition of a heavy and steeply graduated income tax on all incomes over £400 a year, in order to provide comfortable pensions for the aged, the infirm, and widows and orphans, we will have aroused a new spirit in the people; we will have based our revolutionary movement upon a correct appreciation of the needs of the hour, as well as upon the vital principles of economic justice and uncompromising nationality; we will, as the true revolutionist should ever do, have called into action on our side the entire sum of all the forces and factors of social and political discontent. By the use of the revolutionary ballot we will have made the very air of Ireland as laden with 'treason', as fully charged with the spirit of revolt, as it is to-day with the cant of compromise and the mortal sin of flunkeyism; and thus we will have laid a substantial groundwork for more effective action in the future, while to those whom we must remove in our onward march the pledge of our faith in the Social Revolution will convey the assurance that if we crush their profit-making enterprises to-day, yet when the sun dawns upon our freedom, if they have served their fellow creatures loyally in the hour of strife, they and their children and their children's children will be guaranteed against want and privation for all time by the safest guarantee man ever received, the guarantee backed by all the gratitude, the loyal hearts, the brains and industry of the Irish people, under the Irish Socialist Republic.

Industrialism and the Trade Unions

(February 1910)

In the second part of my book *Socialism Made Easy*, I have endeavoured to establish two principles in the minds of my readers as being vitally necessary to the upbuilding of a strong revolutionary Socialist movement. Those two principles are: First, that the working class as a class cannot become permeated with a belief in the unity of their class interests unless they have first been trained to a realization of the need of industrial unity; second, that the revolutionary act – the act of taking over the means of production and establishing a social order based upon the principles of the working class (labour) – cannot be achieved by a disorganized, defeated and humiliated working class, but must be the work of that class after it has attained to a commanding position on the field of economic struggle. It has been a pleasure to me to note the progress of Socialist thought towards acceptance of these principles, and to believe that the publication of that little work helped to a not inconsiderable degree in shaping that Socialist thought and in accelerating its progress. In the following article I wish to present one side of the discussion which inevitably arises in our Socialist party branches upon the mooting of this question. But as a preliminary to this presentation I would like to decry, and ask my comrades to decry and dissociate themselves from, the somewhat acrid and intolerant manner in which this discussion is often carried on. Believing that the Socialist Party is part and parcel of the labour movement of the United States, and that in the growth of that movement to true revolutionary clearness and consciousness it, the Socialist Party, is bound to attract to itself and become mentor and teacher of elements most unclear and lacking in class consciousness, we should recognize that it is as much our duty to be patient and tolerant with the erring brother or sister within our ranks as with the rank heathen – outside the fold. No good purpose can be served by wildly declaiming against 'intellectuals', nor yet by intriguing against and misrepresenting 'impossibilists'. The comrades who think that the Socialist Party is run by 'compromisers' should not jump out of the organization and leave the revolutionists in a still more helpless minority; and the comrades who pride themselves upon being practical Socialist politicians should not too readily accuse those who differ with them of being potential disrupters. Viewing the situation from the standpoint of an industrialist I am convinced that both the industrialist and those estimable comrades who pander to the old style trade unions to such a marked degree as to leave themselves open to the suspicion of coquetting with the idea of a 'labour' party, both, I say, have the one belief, both have arrived at the one conclusion from such different angles that they appear as opposing instead of aiding, auxiliary forces. That belief which both share in common is that the triumph of Socialism is impossible without the aid of labour organized upon the economic field. It is their common possession of this one great principle of action which impels me to say that there is a greater identity of purpose and faith between those two opposing (?) wings of the Socialist Party than either can have with any of the intervening schools of thought. Both realize that the Socialist Party must rest upon the economic struggle and the forces of labour engaged therein, and that the Socialism which is not an outgrowth and expression of that economic struggle is not worth a moment's serious consideration.

There, then, we have found something upon which we agree, a ground common to both, the first desideratum of any serious discussion. The point upon which we disagree is: Can the present form of American trade unions provide the Socialist movement with the economic force upon which to rest, or can the American Federation of Labour develop towards industrialism sufficiently for our needs? It is the same problem stated in different ways. I propose to state here my reasons for taking the negative side in that discussion.

Let it be remembered that we are not, as some good comrades imagine, debating whether it is possible for a member of the American Federation of Labour to become an industrialist, or for all its members, but we are to debate whether the organization of the American Federation of Labour is such as to permit of a modification of its structural formation to keep pace with the progress of industrialist ideas amongst its members. Whether the conversion of the membership of the American Federation of Labour to industrialism would mean the disruption of the Federation and the throwing of it aside as the up-to-date capitalist throws aside a machine, be it ever so costly, when a more perfectly functioning machine has been devised.

At this point it is necessary for the complete understanding of our subject that we step aside for a moment to consider the genesis and organization of the American Federation of Labour and the trade unions patterned after it, and this involves a glance at the history of the labour movement in America. Perhaps of all the subjects properly pertaining to Socialist activity this subject has been the most neglected, the least analysed. And yet it is the most vital. Studies of Marx and popularizing (sic) of Marx, studies of science and popularizing of science, studies of religion and application of same with Socialist interpretations, all these we have without limit. But of attempts to apply the methods of Marx and of science to an analysis of the laws of growth and incidents of development of the organizations of labour upon the economic field the literature of the movement is almost, if not quite, absolutely barren. Our Socialist writers seem in some strange and, to me, incomprehensible manner to have detached themselves from the everyday struggles of the toilers and to imagine they are doing their whole duty as interpreters of Socialist thought when they bless the economic organization with one corner of their mouth and insist upon the absolute hopelessness of it with the other. They imagine, of course, that this is the astutest diplomacy, but the net result of it has been that the organized working class has never looked upon the Socialist Party as a part of the labour movement, and the enrolled Socialist Party member has never found in American Socialist literature anything that helped him in strengthening his economic organization or leading it to victory.

Perhaps some day there will arise in America a Socialist writer who in his writing will live up to the spirit of the *Communist Manifesto* that the Socialists are not apart from the labour movement, are not a sect, but are simply that part of the working class which pushes on all others, which most clearly understands the line of march. Awaiting the advent of that writer, permit me to remind our readers that the Knights of Labour preceded the American Federation of Labour, that the structural formation of the Knights was that of a mass organization, that they aimed to organize all toilers into one union and made no distinction of craft, nor of industry, and that they cherished revolutionary aims. When the American Federation of Labour was organized it was organized as a dual organization, and although at first it professed a desire to organize none but those then unorganized, it soon developed opposition to the Knights and proceeded to organize wherever it could find members, and particularly to seek after the enrolment of those who were already in the Knights of Labour. In this it was assisted by the good will of the master class, who naturally preferred its profession of conservatism and identity of interest between capital and labour to the revolutionary aims and methods of the Knights. But even this assistance on the part of the master class would not have assured its victory were it not for the fact that its method of organization, into separate crafts, recognized a certain need of the industrial development of the time which the Knights of Labour had failed up to that moment to appraise at its proper significance.

The Knights of Labour, as I have pointed out, organized all workers into one union, an excellent idea for teaching the toilers their ultimate class interests, but with the defect that it made no provision for the treating of special immediate craft interests by men and women with the requisite technical knowledge. The scheme was the scheme of an idealist, too large-hearted and noble-minded himself to appreciate the hold small interests can have upon men and women. It gave rise to jealousies. The printer grumbled at the jurisdiction of a body comprising tailors and shoemakers over his shop struggles, and the tailors and shoemakers fretted at the attempts of carpenters and bricklayers to understand the technicalities of their disputes with the bosses.

To save the Knights of Labour and to save the American working class a pilgrimage in the desert of reaction, it but required the advent of some practical student of industry to propose that, instead of massing all workers together irrespective of occupation, they should, keeping the organization intact and remaining bound in obedience to one supreme head, for administrative purposes only, group all workers together according to their industries, and subdivide their industries again according to crafts. That the allied crafts should select the ruling body for the industry to which they belonged, and that the allied industries again should elect the ruling body for the whole organization. This could have been done without the slightest jar to the framework of the organization; it would have recognized all technical differences and specialization of function in actual industry; it would have kept the organization of labour in line with the actual progress of industrial development; and would still have kept intact the idea of the unity of the working class by its common bond of brotherhood, a universal membership card, and universal obligation to recognize that an injury to one was an injury to all.

Tentative steps in such a direction were already being taken when the American Federation of Labour came upon the scene. The promoters of this organization, seizing upon this one plank in the Knights of Labour organization, specialized its work along that line, and, instead of hastening to save the unity of the working class on the lines above indicated, they made the growing realization of the need of representation of craft differences the entering wedge for disrupting and destroying the earlier organization of that class.

Each craft was organized as a distinct body having no obligation to strike or fight beside any other craft, and making its own contracts with the bosses heedless of what was happening between these bosses and their fellow-labourers of another craft in the same industry, building, shop or room. The craft was organized on a national basis, to be governed by the vote of its members throughout the nation, and with a membership card good only in that craft and of no use to a member who desired to leave one craft in order to follow another. The fiction of national unity was and is still paid homage to, as vice always pays homage to virtue, by annual congresses in which many resolutions are gravely debated, to be forgotten as soon as congress adjourns. But the unifying (?) qualities of this form of organization are best revealed by the fact that the main function of the congress seems to be to provide the cynical master class with the, to them, pleasing spectacle of allied organizations fiercely fighting over questions of jurisdiction.

This policy of the American Federation of Labour coupled with the unfortunate bomb incident of Chicago, for which the Knights of Labour received much of the blame, completed the ruin of the latter organization and destroyed the growing unity of the working class for the time being. The industrial union, as typified today in the Industrial Workers of the World, could have, as I have shown, developed out of the Knights of Labour as logically and perfectly as the adult develops from the child. No new organization would have been necessary, and hence we may conclude that the Industrial Workers of the World is the legitimate heir of the native American labour movement, the inheritor of its principles, and the ripened fruit of its experiences. On the other hand the American Federation of Labour may truly be regarded as a usurper on the throne of labour, a usurper who occupies the throne by virtue of having strangled its predecessor, and now, like all usurpers, raises the cry of "treason" against the rightful heir when it seeks to win its own again. It is obvious that the sway of the American Federation of Labour in the American labour movement is but a brief interregnum between the passing of the old revolutionary organization and the ascension into power of the new.

But, I fancy I hear some one say, granting that all that is true, may we not condemn the methods by which the American Federation of Labour destroyed, or helped to destroy, the Knights of Labour, and still believe that out of the American Federation of Labour we may now build up an industrial organization such as we need, such as the Industrial Workers of the World aims to be?

This we can only answer by clearly focusing in our mind the American Federation of Labour system of organization in actual practice. A carpenter is at work in a city. He has a dispute with the bosses, or all his fellow-carpenters have. They will hold meetings to discuss the question of a strike, and finding the problem too big for them they will pass it on to the headquarters, and the headquarters pass it on to the general membership. The general membership, from San Francisco to Rhode Island, and from Podunk to Kalamazoo, will have a vote and say upon the question of the terms upon which the Chicago carpenters work, and if said carpenters are called out they will expect all these widely scattered carpenters to support them by financial and moral help. But while they are soliciting and receiving the support of their fellow-carpenters they are precluded from calling out in sympathy with them the painters who follow them in their work, the plumbers whose pipes they cover up, the steamfitters who work at their elbows, or the plasterer who precedes them. Yet the co-operation of these workers with them in their strikes is a thousandfold more important than the voting of strike funds which would keep them out on strike – until the building season is over and the winter sets in. In many cities today there is a Building Trades' Council which is looked upon by many as a beginning of industrialism within the American Federation of Labour. It is not only the beginning but it is as far as industrialism can go within that body, and its sole function is to secure united action in remedying petty grievances and enforcing the observance of contracts, but it does not take part in the really important work of determining hours or wages. It cannot for the simple reason that each of the thirty-three unions in the building industry are international organizations with international officers, and necessitating international referendums before any strikes, looking to the fixing of hours or wages, are permissible. Hence, although all the building trade branches in a given district may be satisfied that the time is ripe for obtaining better conditions, they cannot act before they obtain the consent of the membership throughout the entire country, and before that is obtained the moment for action is passed. The bond that is supposed to unite the carpenter in New York with the carpenter in Kokomo, Indiana, is converted into a wall of isolation which prevents him uniting, except in the most perfunctory fashion, with the men of other crafts who work beside him. The industrial union and the craft union are mutually exclusive terms. Suppose all the building trades branches of Chicago resolved to unite industrially to form an industrial union. Every branch which became an integral part of said union, pledged to obey its call to action, would by so doing forfeit its charter in the craft union and in the American Federation of Labour, and outside Chicago its members would be considered as scabs. The Brewers Union has been fighting for years to obtain the right to organize all brewery employees. It is hindered from doing so, not only by the rules of the American Federation of Labour, but by the form of organization of that body. Breweries, for instance, employ plumbers. Now if a plumber, so employed, would join the Brewers Union and obey its call to strike he would be expelled from his craft union, and if he ever lost his job in the brewery would be considered as a scab if he went to work where union plumbers were employed. A craft union cannot recognize the right of another association to call its members out on a strike. A machinist works today in a machine shop; a few months from now he may be employed in a clothing factory attending to the repairs of sewing machines. If the clothing industry resolves itself into an industrial union and he joins them, as he needs must if he believes in industrialism, he loses his membership in the International Association of Machinists. And if ever he loses his factory job and seeks to return to the machine shop he must either do so as a non-union man or pay a heavy fine if he is permitted to re-enter the International Association of Machinists. A stationary engineer works today at the construction of a new building, three months from now he is in a shipyard, six months from now he is at the mouth of a coal mine. Three different industries, requiring three different industrial unions.

The craft card is good today in all of them, but if any of them chose to form industrial unions, and called upon him to join, he could only do so on penalty of losing his craft card and his right to strike benefits from his old organization. And if he did join, his card of membership in the one he joined would be of no value when he drifted to any of the others. How can the American Federation of Labour avoid this dilemma? Industrialism requires that all the workers in a given industry be subject to the call of the governing body, or of the vote of the workers in that industry. But if these workers are organized in the American Federation of Labour they must be subject only to the call of their national or international craft body; and if at any time they obey the call of the industry in preference to the craft they are ordered peremptorily back to scab upon their brothers.

If in addition to this organic difficulty, and it is the most insuperable, we take into consideration the system of making contracts or trade agreements on a craft basis pursued by old style unions we will see that our unfortunate brothers in the American Federation of Labour are tied hand and foot, handcuffed and hobbled, to prevent their advance into industrialism. During the regent shirt-waist makers' strike in New York when the question was mooted of a similar strike in Philadelphia our comrade Rose Pastor Stokes, according to our Socialist press, was continually urging upon the shirt-waist makers of Philadelphia the wisdom of striking before Christmas, and during the busy season. No more sensible advice could have been given. It was of the very essence of industrialist philosophy. Industrialism is more than a method of organization – it is a science of fighting. It says to the worker: fight only at the time you select, never when the boss wants a fight. Fight at the height of the busy season, and in the slack season when the workers are in thousands upon the sidewalk absolutely refuse to be drawn into battle. Even if the boss insults and vilifies your union and refuses to recognize it, take it lying down in the slack season but mark it up in your little note book. And when work is again rushing and master capitalist is pressed for orders squeeze him, and squeeze him till the most sensitive portion of his anatomy, his pocket-book, yells with pain. That is the industrialist idea of the present phase of the class war as organized labour should conduct it. But, whatever may have been the case with the shirt-waist makers, that policy so ably enunciated by comrade Rose Pastor Stokes is utterly opposed to the whole philosophy and practice of the American Federation of Labour. Contracts almost always expire when there is little demand for labour. For instance the United Mine Workers' contract with the bosses expires in the early summer when they have before them a long hot season with a minimum demand for coal. Hence the expiration of the contract generally finds the coal operators spoiling for a fight, and the union secretly dreading it. Most building trade contracts with the bosses expire in the winter. For example, the Brotherhood of Carpenters in New York, their contract expires in January. A nice time for a fight, in the middle of a northern winter, when all work in their vicinity is suspended owing to the rigours of the climate!

The foregoing will, I hope, give the reader some food for consideration upon the problem under review. That problem is intimately allied with the future of the Socialist Party in America. Our party must become the political expression of the fight in the workshop, and draw its inspiration therefrom. Everything which tends to strengthen and discipline the hosts of labour tends irresistibly to swell the ranks of the revolutionary movement, and everything which tends to divide and disorganize the hosts of labour tends also to strengthen the forces of capitalism. The most dispersive and isolating force at work in the labour movement today is craft unionism, the most cohesive and unifying force, industrial unionism. In view of that fact all objections which my comrades make to industrial unionism on the grounds of the supposedly, or truly, antipolitical bias of many members of the Industrial Workers of the World is quite beside the mark. That question at the present stage of the game is purely doctrinaire. The use or non-use of political action will not be settled by the doctrinaires who may make it their hobby today, but will be settled by the workers who use the Industrial Workers of the World in their workshop struggles. And if at any time the conditions of a struggle in shop, factory, railroad or mine necessitate the employment of political action those workers so organized will use it, all theories and theorists to the contrary notwithstanding. In their march to freedom the workers will use every weapon they find necessary.

As the economic struggle is the preparatory school and training ground for Socialists it is our duty to help guide along right lines the effort of the workers to choose the correct kind of organization to fight their battles in that conflict. According as they choose aright or wrongly, so will the development of class consciousness in their minds be hastened or retarded by their everyday experience in class struggles.

Sweatshops Behind the Orange Flag

(March 1911)

"For nearly a century the question of Home Government has barred with triple steel every door of progress. It has paralysed the energies of the country, and diverted the currents of national activity into the unfruitful charmers of incessant political struggle. But, indeed, it could not fail to be otherwise. For a hundred years the vast body of the Irish people had neither sympathy with, nor confidence in, the executive and administrative government of Ireland. That Government has no natural root in the soil of Ireland. Bureaucratic government cannot soar on ampler wings. Forty-two Boards, without corelation or connection, and almost without responsibility, control the destinies of Ireland."

The above extract from the manifesto of Ulster Liberal Protestants, issued on 5th December, 1910, will serve as a text for my article this week. I would especially direct the attention of the thoughtful reader to the opening phrase in the quotation. "For nearly a century the question of Home Government has barred with triple steel every door of progress." How true this is every one acquainted with the inner life of Ireland – its civic and social life as distinguished from its political partisanship – can testify. Ireland is a land of contradictions. Just as it is true that the perfervid orators of the United Irish League, who screech most vehemently for national freedom are in domestic affairs in Ireland the allies and champions of social reaction, and the enemies of intellectual freedom, so also it is true that true blue loyalist leaders, who on every platform assert their unquenchable enthusiasm for the cause of Protestant liberty, are the slimiest enemies of the social advancement of the Protestant working class. It may be news to some of your readers, but it is an undoubted fact that the Catholic labourers in the Catholic districts of Ulster reap the advantage of the Acts empowering Boards of Guardians to erect labourers' cottages to a degree far in excess of any advantage given to the Protestant agricultural labourers in the Protestant districts. The enemies of Home Rule and Popery are, it appears, also enemies of low rents and sanitary cottages for their labourers. Where his mind is not obsessed with the fear of compromising the national demand, the Irish Catholic labourer seems to be enough of a democrat to insist upon his social rights as against his Catholic employer or representative; but his Protestant fellow-worker in the north seemingly allows a blatant parade of loyalty to "our Protestant institutions" to compensate for all manner of treachery to the cause of labour.

I have pointed out before that the harmless Act to empower a public provision for the feeding of necessitous school children was kept out of Ireland with the connivance – if not directly at the desire – of the Home Rule Party. Let me add that the Ulster beaters of the Orange drum were equally guilty in that respect. Public meetings to demand the application of this Act to Ireland have already been held in Dublin and Cork. The Dublin Trades' Council has acted, a general committee composed of representatives from the Socialist Party of Ireland, the Daughters of Erin, and the Trades Council have held a public meeting in the Mansion House in furtherance of this object, and induced the Lord Mayor of the city to preside in person; and the Dublin Corporation have unanimously passed a resolution calling for this Act for Ireland. But Belfast and 'Derry have not moved, the Orange orators are too busy dancing imaginary war dances on the banks of the Boyne to trouble about the starving children of Belfast, or of the city by the Foyle.

The Corporation of Catholic Cork granted me the use of their City Hall for a public meeting for this purpose, as have also the Urban

District Council at Queenstown. But the cries of the starving children of Ulster cannot pierce the loyal ears attuned to the after-dinner oratorical efforts of Mr. McMordie, or the poisonous, religious, rancorous ravings of Sir Edward Carson.

But perhaps it will be argued that the prosperity of Belfast is so great that such an Act would be quite unnecessary, and did not Mr. McMordie rise in his place in the House of Commons and work in a free advertisement for workers in the linen trade of that city, by telling of the great demand for workers there, and of its great and abundant prosperity. I extract from the *Belfast Newsletter*, a rabidly loyalist paper, of September 8, 1910, the following short report of a speech delivered in the Ulster Hall, Belfast, by Miss Mary Galway, Secretary of the Millworkers, on the conditions of sweated outworkers in the linen industry in Belfast. It shows how the Godly Protestant employers of Belfast sweat and rob the Godly Protestant workers, and how zeal for the Empire is made a cloak to trick out a mad desire to amass wealth by grinding the faces of the poor:

"Miss Galway then displayed samples of the work done in the home, and gave figures regarding the rate of pay. She said for clipping cotton pocket handkerchiefs with 120 clips on each a sum of 1d. per dozen was paid, and it took an expert worker five hours to clip twelve dozen. For threaddrawing pure linen handkerchiefs supplied by one of the best and oldest firms in the city, 1d. per dozen was paid, and six dozen could be drawn in one hard day's work. A widow with seven children could earn at most 4/- per week at hand-spoke work, the rate of payment being 1/3 per dozen handkerchiefs. For clipping the threads on an elaborately embroidered bedspread, 88 ins. by 100 ins., 3/4d. was paid, and it took fully an hour to do that work. Another woman was engaged three long days embroidering a linen teacloth, 45 ins. by 43 ins., for which she was paid 8d. Thread-drawing of pillow-cases was paid at the rate of 4d. per dozen, and four could be done in an hour. On a cotton handkerchief there were 112 dots, and the worker was paid 6d. per dozen handerchiefs, while at shirtmaking an expert worker could earn about 1/3 in fourteen hours. She could quote other instances showing the long hours and wretched pay of these workers, and yet they were asked was there any sweating?"

Since then, in answer to his unctuous self-congratulations in Parliament, Miss Galway has challenged Mr. M'Mordie, M.P., to take a walk with her to houses within fifteen minutes of the Belfast City Hall, and she would show him still more outrageous cases of sweating; but no acceptance is yet forthcoming.

But when election time rolls around, the smug representative of orangeism will beat the big drum of "saving the union" before the working class voters, and with that discord in their ears they will be deaf to the cry of the helpless victims of capitalist oppression.

Oh, words of burning truth! "For nearly a century the question of Home Government has barred with triple steel every door of progress!"

The question of Home Government, the professional advocacy of it, and the professional opposition to it, is the greatest asset in the hands of reaction in Ireland, the never-failing decoy to lure the workers into the bogs of religious hatreds and social stagnation.

The Protestant workers of Belfast are essentially democratic in their instincts, but not a single Belfast loyalist M.P. voted for the Old Age Pensions' Act. The loyalist M.P.s knew that the beating of the orange drum would drown every protest within their constituencies.

The development of democracy in Ireland has been smothered by the Union. Remove that barrier, throw the Irish people back upon their own resources, make them realise that the causes of poverty, of lack of progress, of arrested civic and national development, are then to be sought for within and not without, are in their power to remove or perpetuate, and ere long that spirit of democratic progress will invade and permeate all our social and civic institutions.

Believing that that day is approaching, the Socialist Party of Ireland seeks to prepare for it by laying now the foundations of that socialist movement, whose duty it will be to guide and direct the efforts of labour in Ireland, to find and fashion a proper channel of expression and instrument of emancipation.

That labour movement of the future, as well as the socialist movement of today must, indeed, draw inspiration from the successes of our comrades abroad, but must also shape its course to suit the conditions within our own shores.

The Socialist Party of Ireland recognises and most enthusiastically endorses the principle of internationalism, but it realises that that principle must be sought through the medium of universal brotherhood rather than by self-extinction of distinct nations within the political maw of over-grown Empires.

When once all the socialists in Ireland recognise this principle, and unite with us, they will have cause to wonder at the readiness with which the workers of Ireland will respond to the socialist appeal.

If all the socialists in Ireland who waste their time in cursing the unprogressiveness of the Irish workers, had only sufficient moral courage to declare themselves, they would be astonished at the multitude of their numbers, and would then realise that they were strong enough to ensure respect and toleration.

Until they do, we will be compelled to see Irish Tory employers hiding their sweatshops behind orange flags, and Irish home rule landlords using the green sunburst of Erin to cloak their rackrenting in the festering slums of our Irish towns.

Direct Action in Belfast

(September 1911)

We have just had, and taken, the opportunity in Belfast to put into practice a little of what is known on the Continent of Europe as 'Direct Action'.

Direct Action consists in ignoring all the legal and parliamentary ways of obtaining redress for the grievances of Labour, and proceeding to rectify these grievances by direct action upon the employer's most susceptible part – his purse. This is very effective at times, and saves much needless worry, and much needless waste of union funds.

Direct Action is not liked by lawyers, politicians, or employers. It keeps the two former out of a job, and often leaves the latter out of pocket. But it is useful to Labour, and if not relied upon too exclusively, or used too recklessly, it may yet be made a potent weapon in the armoury of the working class.

The circumstances under which we came to put in practice the newest adaptation of it in Belfast were as follows:

A dock labourer named Keenan was killed at the unloading of a ship owing to a bag being released by one of the carriers a moment too soon. Flying down the chute it struck Keenan, knocking him to the ground and killing him. The accident happened owing to the practice of the stevedores of backing in a team of horses about ten minutes before the meal hour, and demanding that the men rush the work in order to load the vans before quitting for their meals. It was in this perfectly needless rush the sad affair happened.

What was our surprise to read in the report of the inquest that the solicitor for the merchant insinuated that the man was killed because he was a non-union man – that in short he was murdered by the union members! As a matter of fact he had promised to join, and being an old dock labourer had been given a few days grace in which to come up to our offices and make good.

All the papers of Belfast gave prominence to this "Extraordinary Allegation", as one journal called it, and the matter was commented upon freely throughout the city.

After due deliberation, thinking over all the possible means of redress for this foul libel we resolved to take the matter into our own hands, and put a little pressure upon the purse of the man who employed this libeller to slander the Union.

Accordingly at dinner time we told the men employed on the ship in question – the *Nile* – not to resume work until the merchant repudiated the libel or disclaimed all responsibility therefor. The men stood by loyally, and immediately all the forces of capital and law and order were on the alert. The news spread around the docks as on a wireless telegraph, and both sides were tense with expectancy.

While we were thus waiting and watching the stevedore of the *Nile* sent for the merchant, and asked me through one of his foremen to wait on the spot for him. I waited, but whilst I waited one very officious Harbour official ordered me off the Harbour Estate. The Harbour of Belfast, unlike Dublin or Liverpool, is practically enclosed property. I informed Mr Constable that there was no meeting in progress, and that I was only waiting an answer to our request for a disclaimer from the merchant. He then became rude and domineering, and eventually began to use force. I then told him that if I, as a union official, could not speak to the men individually on the Harbour Estate we would take the men off where we could talk to them.

So we gave the word and called off every man in the Low Docks. In ten minutes 600 men responded and left the docks empty.

In ten minutes more a District Superintendent, merchants, managers, detectives, and Harbour underlings generally were rushing frantically up to the Union rooms begging for the men to go back and "everything would be arranged."

Well, everything was arranged within an hour. The offending solicitor, after many hoity-toity protests that "he would not be dictated to by the dockers," climbed gracefully down and dictated a letter to the Press disclaiming any intention to impute evil actions to the Union members, and the letter accordingly appeared in all the Belfast papers.

In addition the Harbour Master assured us that he regretted the action of the constable, which would not be allowed to happen again, and that we would be given full liberty to go anywhere in the docks or ships at all times.

It was all a great object lesson, and has had its full effect on the minds of the Belfast workers. It has taught them that there are other ways than by means of expensive law-suits to vindicate the character and rights of the toilers; and as a result it has given dignity and self-respect to the members of the Union.

We have found it necessary, in order to cope with the needs of our increasing membership, to open new offices for the Ballymacarret side of the city. These offices are at 6 Dalton Street, and will be in charge of a Union official between the hours of 4 and 7 p.m. during the week, and from 12 to 5 p.m. on Saturdays. They will be a great convenience to the local Quay and to our new members from the Chemical Works.

Our campaign against the sweating conditions in the Rope Works is now in full swing. Breakfast and dinner hour meetings are being held when the gospel of discontent and wise organisation is preached to the sweated employees of this huge capitalist concern. We expect good results to the workers from this campaign.

On Tuesday, September 11th, we held a most successful joint demonstration with the seamen and firemen, with Father Hopkins as our chief speaker. The magnitude of the meeting surprised and delighted our comrade, and his speech surprised and delighted the vast audience.

Mr D.R. Campbell, President Belfast Trades Council, was in the chair, and the following resolution was moved by James Connolly, seconded by James Flanagan, supported by Father Hopkins, and passed amid great enthusiasm:

Resolved – "That in the opinion of this meeting of Belfast workers, the action of Wexford employers in discharging men for joining the Irish Transport Workers' Union was an outrageous attack upon the liberty of the workers; and that we call upon our Wexford brothers to stand firm, and also call upon all trade unionists in Ireland to answer this outrage by boycotting all the bicycles and other products manufactured by the firm in question."

The meeting closed with ringing cheers for Father Hopkins, singing of He's a jolly good fellow, and cheers for the Transport Workers' Union.

British Labour and Irish Politicians

(May, 1913)

I have spent a great portion of my life alternating between interpreting Socialism to the Irish and interpreting the Irish to the Socialists. Of the two tasks, I confess, that while I am convinced that the former has been attended with a considerable degree of success, the latter has not. At least as far as the Socialists of Great Britain are concerned, they always seem to me to exhibit towards the Irish working-class democracy of the Labour movement the same inability to understand their position and to share in their aspirations as the organised British nation, as a whole, has shown to the struggling Irish nation it has so long held in subjection.

No one, and least of all the present writer, would deny the sympathy of the leaders of the British Labour movement towards the Labour and Socialist movements of Ireland, but a sympathy not based upon understanding is often more harmful than a direct antagonism. A case in point will serve to illustrate my meaning as well as to provide a guide and a warning for the future.

Upon the passing of the Local Government Act, establishing household suffrage for the municipalities and local governing bodies of Ireland, in 1898, the Trades Councils and other trades bodies all over this country proceeded to form independent Labour Electoral

Associations for the purpose of running Labour candidates against the nominees of both the orthodox Irish political parties.

At once, as was natural, the capitalist politicians took fright, and in press and on platform the Irish workers were denounced for daring to abandon their 'natural leaders'.

But the Irish workers who knew the Irish political cliques and their leaders at first hand and appraised them accordingly at their just value, went on with the nomination of their candidates, practically every trades council in this country being actively engaged in the work of fighting for independent Labour representation.

The small British Socialist press which then existed had given, up till this, a cordial approval of this hopeful development of the political side of the Irish Labour movement.

But so ominous did this movement appear to the interests which control the Home Rule party that eventually the present leader of that party took the field against it, and in a carefully reported speech, declared that 'Labour and Nationality must march together', meaning as all his hearers knew, as everybody in Ireland knew, that Labour must abandon its political adventure as a separate cause, and must be content to seek its fortunes as a subordinate issue in the Home Rule camp.

Labour, in Ireland, did not pay much attention to this pronouncement against it, but the responsible leaders of the Labour movement in Great Britain immediately seized upon this phrase and in press and on platform it was heralded in that country as a 'magnificent pronouncement of the Irish party in favour of Labour'.

In the *Workers' Republic,* March, 1901, and October, 1901, Connolly made similar criticisms of the British Labour attitude; in his final article he wrote: "Mr. Keir Hardie, MP, and his colleagues on the Labour Leader have been assiduously instilling into the minds of the British Socialists the belief that Mr. John Redmond's Home Rule Party are burning with enthusiasm for Labour and are favourably inclined towards Socialism. We beg our readers in Ireland not to laugh at this ... We do not agree with Hardie's general policy, would decidedly not adopt it as our own, but we believe in his honesty of purpose. We ask nothing from the English democracy but we do not wish to cross one another's path. We believe the Irish working class are strong enough to fight their own battles and we would be the last to advise them to seek outside help in the struggle that lies before them. We do not propose to criticise Hardie's voting alliance with the Home Rulers, but a voting alliance need not be accompanied by indiscriminate praise of your temporary allies." In his first article Connolly wrote: "The Irish Home Rule party is essentially a capitalist party ... Its chiefs do indeed 'recognise that there is a Labour question', but they recognise it only in order to sidetrack and postpone indefinitely its discussion."

A more ridiculous perversion of facts it would be hard to conceive. But all during these fiercely contested Local Government elections in Ireland where Irish MP's were brought down in shoals into the municipal wards to fight against the nominees of the Irish Trade Unions, these same MP's had no better weapons in their armouries than the eulogies which, in England, were being lavished by responsible Labour men upon the Home Rule leaders – eulogies based upon and only made possible by a wresting of the language of a politician from all relation to the circumstances which inspired it.

If some one had said, in England, that "Labour and Liberalism must march together", no one would have or could have construed it into a declaration of Liberalism in favour of the Labour movement, but all would have recognised it as a declaration against that political independence of Labour which is the very essence of the movement. So it was with the former declaration in Ireland; but the British Socialists, accustomed to think of the Home Rule party as a minority party, utterly misunderstood its attitude and language when speaking in Ireland as a majority party deprecating all political activities not under the control of its officials.

This is but one sample out of many that could be quoted of the difficulty of making the comrades in Great Britain understand the totally different conditions in Ireland and also understand that these conditions naturally produce catch-words, phrases and rallying cries which bear no relation to the conditions which prevail in Great Britain.

The Labour party in Parliament tries to surmount this difficulty by, so to speak, establishing Home Rule in its relations with Ireland. Thus, if a trade union in Ireland writes to the Labour party asking that a certain question be raised in Parliament, if that question pertains to a district represented by a member of the Home Rule party, the answer sent to the trade union generally is that the question has been turned over to the Irish party, and that should that Party raise it in the House, the Labour Party will support it.

As the Irish Parliamentary Party desires to pose in Ireland as opposed to all class division, and as a cold matter of fact is generally bossed locally by small sweating employers, slum landlords and publicans, the MP from the district never brings the question up and the incident never is made public, but only serves to accentuate "the pleasant relations which exist in the House between the Irish Party and Labour". Ahem!

As a result of these "pleasant relations", there was no one in the House to fight for the inclusion of Ireland in the Meals for Necessitous School Children Act and thus while reformers in England are now fiercely fighting for the right to feed children during holidays, the school children of Ireland are yet denied the primary right of being fed during school hours.

A threat from the Labour Party to wreck the Insurance Bill unless Ireland was included in the Medical Benefits would have secured that, the best part of the Act, for Ireland. But that would have disturbed the pleasant relations also, and Ireland was left out, and a totally inadequate, unworkable Act without that provision foisted upon this country.

Ireland is, to-day, the battle-ground almost daily of fierce industrial disputes. In these disputes there are continual outrages by a police and constabulary over whom no popularly elected body in city or country exercises the smallest control; but in no case are these outrages upon Labour made the subject of Parliamentary questions by the Irish parties. Strikers arrested in industrial disputes are tried and sentenced by resident magistrates drawn entirely from the possessing classes; but although their findings and sentences are usually a travesty upon law and an outrage upon justice, the smug serenity of our lawmakers is never troubled by any question pertaining thereto.

Labour and Nationality, now as in 1898, are marching together (in Parliament) and the fierce battles of the labourer in the towns of Ireland for bread must not disturb their pleasant relations.

Oh yes, the Home Rulers are great democrats – in England; great friends of Labour – in England; heroic defenders of the common people – in England. But in Ireland. Ah! that is another matter.

During a lock-out in Dundalk at the beginning of last year, a girl picket was arrested for striving to induce another girl not to blackleg. She was summarily tried and sentenced to prison on a charge of "indecent conduct in the streets". No unclean language or action had been attributed to her and the police evidence simply stated that she had persisted in picketing, yet the cold-blooded scoundrelism of the authorities framed a charge against her calculated to blast her character and ruin her whole life. If she had been a daughter of an Irish farmer fighting an Irish landlord in Land League days the then Irish Party would have made the world ring with their denunciations of such character assassinations; but she was only an Irish working girl fighting an Irish employer, and none of the Irish heroes who, on the platforms of the Liberal Party in England, are fighting for the "Glory of God and the Honour of Erin", had time to waste on such as her.

Small wonder that we in Ireland are working to establish a Labour Party of our own. We have no fault to find with the Labour Party in Great Britain. We recognise that it has its own problems to face and that it cannot well be expected to turn aside to grapple with ours. And, Heaven knows, these problems are serious enough to require the most earnest study and undivided attention of men on the spot. They require more study and attention than can be given by men absorbed in the urgent problems of the greater population across the water.

From time to time I propose to give some attention to the elucidation of the problems peculiar to Ireland and particularly to this part of it. For the present, it is sufficient to emphasise the fact that the religious affiliations of the population of Ulster determine their political leanings to a greater extent than is the case in any part of Europe outside the Balkans. But the manner in which this has developed is also unique. I believe that it is true to say that, politically speaking, the Protestantism of the North of Ireland has no parallel outside this country, and that the Catholicism of the Irish Catholics is, likewise, peculiar in its political trend.

To explain – I mean that, whereas, Protestantism has in general made for political freedom and political Radicalism, it has been opposed to slavish worship of kings and aristocrats. Here, in Ireland, the word Protestant is almost a convertible term with Toryism, lickspittle loyalty, servile worship of aristocracy and hatred of all that savours of genuine political independence on the part of the 'lower classes'.

And in the same manner, Catholicism which in most parts of Europe is synonymous with Toryism, lickspittle loyalty, servile worship of aristocracy and hatred of all that savours of genuine political independence on the part of the lower classes, in Ireland is almost synonymous with rebellious tendencies, zeal for democracy, and intense feeling of solidarity with all strivings upward of those who toil.

Such a curious phenomenon is easily understood by those who know the history of Ireland. Unfortunately for their spiritual welfare – and I am using the word 'spiritual', not in its theological but in its better significance as controlling mental and moral development upward – the Protestant elements of Ireland were, in the main, a plantation of strangers upon the soil from which the owners had been dispossessed by force. The economic dispossession was, perforce, accompanied by a political and social outlawry. Hence every attempt of the dispossessed to attain citizenship, to emerge from their state of outlawry, was easily represented as a tentative step towards reversing the plantation and towards replanting the Catholic and dispossessing the Protestant.

Imagine this state of matters persisting for over 200 years and one realises at once that the planted population – the Protestants – were bound to acquire insensibly a hatred of political reform, and to look upon every effort of the Catholic to achieve political recognition as an insidious move towards the expulsion of Protestants. Then the Protestant always saw that the kings and aristocrats of England and Ireland were opposed by the people whom he most feared and from recognising that it was but an easy step to regard his cause as identical with theirs. They had a common enemy, and he began to teach his children that they had a common cause, and common ideals.

This is the reason – their unfortunate isolation as strangers holding a conquered country in fee for rulers alien to its people – that the so-called Scotch of Ulster have fallen away from and developed antagonism to political reform and mental freedom as rapidly as the Scots of Scotland have advanced in adhesion to these ideals.

The Catholics, for their part, and be it understood I am talking only of the Catholic workers, have been as fortunately placed for their political education as they were unfortunately placed for their political and social condition. Just as the Socialist knows that the working class, being the lowest in the social system, cannot emancipate itself without as a result emancipating all other classes, so the Irish Catholic has realised instinctively that he, being the most oppressed and disfranchised, could not win any modicum of political freedom or social recognition for himself without winning it for all others in Ireland. Every upward step of the Catholic has emancipated some one of the smaller Protestant sects; every successful revolt of the Catholic peasant has given some added security even to those Protestant farmers who were most zealously defending the landlord. And out of this struggle the Catholic has, perforce, learned toleration. He has learned that his struggle is, and has been, the struggle of all the lowly and dispossessed, and he has grown broad-minded with the broad-mindedness of the slave in revolt against slavery.

But with the advent of Home Rule, nay even with the promise of Home Rule and the entrance of Ireland upon the normal level of civilised, self-governing nations, the old relation of Protestant and Catholic begins to melt and dissolve, and with their dissolution will come a new change in the relation of either faith to politics. The loss of its privileged position will mean for Protestantism the possibilities of an immense spiritual uplifting; an emergence into a knowledge of its kinship with its brothers and sisters of different creeds. Whether the entrance of Catholicity into a position of mere numerical voting power will lead, in its turn, to a withering up of those kindly feelings born of its past sufferings is another matter. I do not believe that it will, at least amongst the toilers. Our apprenticeship to misery has been too long, our journeyings in the desert of slavery have surely implanted in our breasts a sense of the criminality of any attempt to impose fetters upon others such as we have ourselves worn. And out of that belief the writer looks forward with confidence to the future, believing that the tale these Notes from Ireland will have to tell will be a hopeful one, even if the hope is nurtured amid storm and stress.

Labour and the Proposed Partition of Ireland

(March 1914)

The recent proposals of Messrs. Asquith, Devlin, Redmond and Co. for the settlement of the Home Rule question deserve the earnest attention of the working class democracy of this country. They reveal in a most striking and unmistakeable manner the depths of betrayal to which the so-called Nationalist politicians are willing to sink. For generations the conscience of the civilised world has been shocked by the historical record of the partition of Poland; publicists, poets, humanitarians, patriots, all lovers of their kind and of progress have wept over the unhappy lot of a country torn asunder by the brute force of their alien oppressors, its unity ruthlessly destroyed and its traditions trampled into the dust.

But Poland was disrupted by outside forces, its enemies were the mercenaries of the tyrant kingdoms and empires of Europe; its sons and daughters died in the trenches and on the battlefields by the thousands rather than submit to their beloved country being annihilated as a nation. But Ireland, what of Ireland? It is the trusted leaders of Ireland that in secret conclave with the enemies of Ireland have agreed to see Ireland as a nation disrupted politically and her children divided under separate political governments with warring interests.

Now, what is the position of Labour towards it all? Let us remember that the Orange aristocracy now fighting for its supremacy in Ireland has at all times been based upon a denial of the common human rights of the Irish people; that the Orange Order was not founded to safeguard religious freedom, but to deny religious freedom, and that it raised this religious question, not for the sake of any religion, but in order to use religious zeal in the interests of the oppressive property rights of rackrenting landlords and sweating capitalists. That the Irish people might be kept asunder and robbed whilst so sundered and divided, the Orange aristocracy went down to the lowest depths and out of the lowest pits of hell brought up the abominations of sectarian feuds to stir the passions of the ignorant mob. No crime was too brutal or cowardly; no lie too base; no slander too ghastly, as long as they served to keep the democracy asunder.

And now that the progress of democracy elsewhere has somewhat muzzled the dogs of aristocratic power, now that in England as well as in Ireland the forces of labour are stirring and making for freedom and light, this same gang of well-fed plunderers of the people, secure in Union held upon their own dupes, seek by threats of force to arrest the march of idea and stifle the light of civilisation and liberty. And, lo and behold, the trusted guardians of the people, the vaunted saviours of the Irish race, agree in front of the enemy and in face of the world to sacrifice to the bigoted enemy the unity of the nation and along with it the lives, liberties and hopes of that portion of the nation which in the midst of the most hostile surroundings have fought to keep the faith in things national and progressive.

Such a scheme as that agreed to by Redmond and Devlin, the betrayal of the national democracy of industrial Ulster would mean a carnival of reaction both North and South, would set back the wheels of progress, would destroy the oncoming unity of the Irish Labour movement and paralyse all advanced movements whilst it endured.

To it Labour should give the bitterest opposition, against it Labour in Ulster should fight even to the death, if necessary, as our fathers fought before us.

Ireland and Ulster: An Appeal to the Working Class

(April 1914)

In this great crisis of the history of Ireland, I desire to appeal to the working class – the only class whose true interests are always on the side of progress – to take action to prevent the betrayal of their interests contemplated by those who have planned the exclusion of part of Ulster from the Home Rule Bill. Every effort is now being made to prevent the voice of the democracy being heard in those counties and boroughs which it is callously proposed to cut off from the rest of Ireland. Meetings are being rushed through in other parts of Ireland, and at those meetings wirepullers of the United Irish League and the Ancient Order of Hibernians (Board of Erin) are passing resolutions approving of the exclusion, whilst you who will suffer by this dastardly proposal are never even consulted, but, on the contrary, these same organisations are working hard to prevent your voice being heard, and have done what they could to prevent the calling of meetings, of holding of demonstrations at which you could register your hatred of their attempt to betray you into the hand of the sworn enemies of democracy, of labour, and of nationality.

An instance of this attempt to misrepresent you may be quoted from the Irish press of March 26. In a letter from the Irish Press Agency it says:

"The proposal, representing the limit of concession and made 'as the price of peace' would only mean, if accepted, that the Counties of Down, Derry, Antrim and Armagh would remain as they are for six years at the end of which time they would come in automatically under Home Rule. They know, too, that the Nationalists in these four counties are perfectly willing to assent to this arrangement and that they are the Nationalists most concerned."

Remember that this is a quotation from a letter sent out by the Irish Press Agency and that copies of it are supplied by the agents of the Irish Parliamentary Party to every newspaper in Ireland and to Liberal papers in England, and you will see how true is my statement that you are being betrayed, that the men whom you trusted are busily engaged in rigging up a fake sentiment in favour of this betrayal of your interests. For the statements contained in the letter just quoted are, in the first part, deliberately misleading and, and in the second part, an outrageous falsehood.

The statement that the counties excluded would come in automatically at the end of six years is deliberately misleading because, as was explained in the House of Commons, two General Elections would take place before the end of that time. If at either of these General Elections the Tories got a majority – and it is impossible to believe that the Liberals can win the other two elections successively – it would only require the passage of a small Act of not more than three or four lines to make the exclusion perpetual. And the Tories would pass it. What could prevent them? You can prevent them getting the chance by insisting upon the whole Home Rule Bill and no exclusion, being passed now. If you do not act now, your chance is gone.

The second part of the statement I have quoted is an outrageous falsehood, as every one knows. The Nationalists of the four counties have not been asked their opinion, and if any politician would dare to take a plebiscite upon this question of exclusion or no exclusion, the democracy of Ulster would undoubtedly register a most emphatic refusal to accept this proposal. And yet so-called Home Rule journals are telling the world that you are quite willing to be cut off from

Ireland and placed under the heel of the intolerant gang of bigots and enemies of progress who for so long have terrorised Ulster.

Men and women, consider! If your lot is a difficult one now, subject as you are to the rule of a gang who keep up the fires of religious bigotry in order to divide the workers, and make united progress impossible; if your lot is a difficult one, even when supported by the progressive and tolerant forces of all Ireland, how difficult and intolerable it will be when you are cut off from Ireland, and yet are regarded as alien to Great Britain, and left at the tender mercies of a class who knows no mercy, of a mob poisoned by ignorant hatred of everything national and democratic.

Do not be misled by the promises of politicians. Remember that Mr. Birrell, Chief Secretary, solemnly promised that a representative of Dublin Labour would sit upon the Police Inquiry Commission in Dublin, and that he broke his solemn promise. Remember that Mr. Redmond pledged his word at Waterford that the Home Rule Bill would go through without the loss of a word or a comma, and almost immediately afterwards he agreed to the loss of four counties and two boroughs. Remember that the whole history of Ireland is a record of betrayals by politicians and statesmen, and remembering this, spurn their lying promises and stand up for a United Ireland – an Ireland broad based upon the union of Labour and Nationality.

You are not frightened by the mock heroics of a pantomime army. Nobody in Ulster is. If the politicians in Parliament pretend to be frightened, it is only in order to find an excuse to sell you. Do not be sold. Remember that when soldiers were ordered out to shoot you down in the Belfast Dock Strike of 1907 no officer resigned then rather than shed blood in Ulster, and when some innocent members of our class were shot down in the Falls Road, Belfast, no Cabinet Ministers apologised to the relatives of the poor workers they had murdered. Remember that more than a thousand Dublin men, women and children were brutally beaten and wounded by the police a few months ago, and three men and one girl killed, but no officer resigned, and neither Tory nor Home Rule press protested against the coercion of Dublin. Why, then, the hypocritical howl against compelling the pious sweaters of Ulster and their dupes to obey the will of the majority? Remember the A.O.H., the U.I.L. and the Irish Parliamentary Party cheered on the Government when it sent its police to bludgeon the Nationalist workers of Dublin. Now the same organisation and the same party cheers on the same treacherous Government when it proposes to surrender you into the hands of the Carsonite gang. As the officers of the Curragh have stood by their class, so let the working-class democracy of Ulster stand by its class and all Irish workers from Malin Head to Cape Clear and from Dublin to Galway will stand by you.

Let your motto be that of James Fintan Lalor, the motto which the working class Irish Citizen Army has adopted as its aim and object, viz.:

That the entire ownership of Ireland [all Ireland] – moral and material – is vested of right in the entire people of Ireland.

And, adopting this as your motto, let it be heard and understood that Labour in Ireland stands for the unity of Ireland – an Ireland united in the name of progress, and who shall separate us?

Independent Labour Party of Ireland: Ireland Upon The Dissecting Table

(April 1914)

Fellow-Workers,

As the only political organisation in the North of Ireland which, seeking first the well-being and freedom of the working class, has yet at all times resolutely stood for the attainment of Irish Nationhood, we desire to appeal to you and the public generally to protest with all possible power and without loss of time against the proposal to allow the unity of Ireland to be placed at the mercy of the voters in a small part of Ireland. The Exclusion Proposals put forward by the Liberal Government and accepted by the Home Rule Party, mean that a vote is to be taken of the electors in the Ulster counties and in the two boroughs of Belfast and Derry on the question of whether these places will continue to be reckoned as part of Ireland, and therefore as subject to the Home Rule Bill. If the majority in any one of these places vote against Home Rule then chat county or borough will be cut off politically from Ireland and the Home Rule Bill will not apply to it. This, in simple language, means that a local majority, in Belfast or Derry, for instance, are to be given the power to wreak their hatred upon Ireland by dismembering her, by cutting Ireland to pieces as a corpse would be cut upon the dissecting table.

Cromwell, in his worst days, the Orange Order in its most atrocious moments, never planned a more dastardly outrage upon the Irish nation than this. And remember that this is planned by the political parties who for a generation have taught you to believe that they hoped for and worked for IRELAND A NATION. Yet in the moment when it was possible and easy to realise that ideal they consented to betray you, and to place your hopes and the unity of your nation at the mercy of the voters in the Ulster counties and boroughs, where the seeds of intolerance, bigotry and opposition to social progress have borne the most evil fruit and darkened the vision of the largest multitudes.

But we will be told that this Exclusion is to be only temporary, and Home Rule and Liberal politicians are whispering into your ears that they are resolutely opposed to any extension of the six years' limit. Do not be misled. Remember that no man can foretell the course of politics. Could any Home Ruler have foretold one year ago that the Home Rule Party would have consented even to discuss this dismemberment of the Irish Nation? He would have been driven in disgrace out of the A.O.H. or the U.I.L., if he had suggested a year ago that such a thing was possible. But today these organisations are loud in their approval of the proposal to put Ireland upon the dissecting table and to give into the hands of Sir Edward Carson and his dupes the knife with which to cut her up. But truth will out, and even the politicians themselves let slip the fact about the real probabilities of the future. Read the speech of Mr. John Dillon, M.P., in the House of Commons on the night of Wednesday, April 1st, as reported in the Liberal *Daily News and Leader* of the following day. He laid stress upon the fact that two General Elections will take place within the six years. He said:

"Ulster had been offered the safeguard of two elections, and it would be an event unparalleled in British history for the Unionist Party not to win one of them."

What would happen then, if the Unionist Party won one of these elections, as Mr. Dillon says they almost certainly would? On the same night the Solicitor-General supplied the answer. He said:

"If the other side came into power and brought forward a Bill to exclude Ulster it would have a royal and triumphal procession to the foot of the throne."

So that here you have two leading spokesmen of the Liberal and Home Rule Parties admitting that the six years' limit is only a form of speech – that in practical politics it will have no real existence. What this proposal is really doing is establishing the right of, and giving the power to, a small minority to destroy the nation as a nation, to – we again repeat it – place Ireland upon the dissecting table, and give into the hands of Sir Edward Carson and his followers the knife with which to cut her up. No amount of speeches against Exclusion which the Home Rule politicians may hereafter make should be allowed to cover or hide their complicity in this damnable crime, or to obscure the fact that it was and is their acceptance of Mr. Asquith's proposal that alone makes Exclusion possible.

Think of all the measures needed by the workers in this part of the country which will be impossible if this Exclusion is allowed. The Nationalisation of Irish Railways, so badly needed, will be an impossibility; the Extension to Ireland of the Medical Benefits of the Insurance Act, the Provision of Meals to Children at School, the Abolition of Sweating, and the general safeguarding of the interests of Mill Workers and other forms of Labour needing Legal Protection, will all be delayed, if not absolutely lost, if any part of Ulster is cut off from Ireland as a nation. And in addition, all the old sectarian jealousies will be kept up, workers will be kept fighting with workers and progress will be impossible.

We appeal to you then to arouse yourselves to the gravity of the occasion. Make your protest in every possible way. Do not allow it to be said of you by the children of the future that your generation was the only generation in all the history of Ireland that consented to betray her, that granted to an intolerant minority the power to destroy the unity of the country to disrupt and dismember it, and that you granted this at the very moment when Labour elsewhere in Ireland was most assertive of its rights and most desirous of a Free Irish Nation as the natural guardian of those rights.

EXECUTIVE COMMITTEE, Independent Labour Party of Ireland, Belfast Branch

The Problem of Trade Union Organization

(May 1914).

Recently I have been complaining in this column and elsewhere of the tendency in the Labour movement to mistake mere concentration upon the industrial field for essentially revolutionary advance. My point was that the amalgamation or federation of unions, unless carried out by men and women with the proper revolutionary spirit, was as likely to create new obstacles in the way of effective warfare, as to make that warfare possible. The argument was reinforced by citations of what is taking place in the ranks of the railwaymen and in the transport industry. There we find that the amalgamations and federations are rapidly becoming engines for steam-rollering or suppressing all manifestations of revolutionary activity, or effective demonstrations of brotherhood. Every appeal to take industrial action on behalf of a union in distress is blocked by insisting upon the necessity of "first obtaining the sanction of the Executive", and in practice it is found that the process of obtaining that sanction is so long, so cumbrous, and surrounded with so many rules and regulations that the union in distress is certain to be either disrupted or bankrupted before the Executive can be moved. The Greater Unionism is found in short to be forging greater fetters for the working class; to bear to the real revolutionary industrial unionism the same relation as the servile State would bear to the Co-operative Commonwealth of our dreams.

This argument of mine, which to many people may appear as far-fetched, gains new strength from the circumstances related by our friend Robert Williams of the Transport Workers Federation, in the weekly report of that body for the 9 May. After describing how the Head Line Company played with the above Federation in connection with its protest against the continued victimization of the members of the Irish Transport Workers Union, and how he was powerless to effect anything as the other unions involved still continued to work the scab ships, he goes on to tell of a similar state of affairs in the Port of London. The quotation is long, but it is so valuable an instructive lesson to all your readers that I do not hesitate to give it as an ample confirmation of my argument.

"This week, again, there has been a recrudescence of the trouble existing between the Seamen's Union at Tilbury and the Anglo-American Oil Company. This Company has a fleet of oil-tank steamers running between America and various ports in this country.

"As a result of the protest made by the crew of the SS *Narragansett* against the chief steward, who acted in the most inhumane manner towards one of the crew who received a severe injury, this Company displaced union men and took on Shipping Federation scabs. Further than this, they have replaced all union men by obtaining Federation scabs in ship after ship since the commencement of the trouble. On Sunday last the *Narragansett* arrived once more at Purfleet, on the lower reaches of the Thames, and the Tilbury Secretary of the Seamen's Union, Mr E. Potton, naturally commenced to hustle. He communicated with Mr Harry Gosling, Mr Havelock Wilson, and the Secretary of this Federation, in order, if possible, to bring pressure upon the Company by preventing the ship from being bunkered.

"After consultation with Messrs Gosling and Wilson, the Secretary telephoned, and further, wrote the Anglo-American Oil Company asking them to confer with one or more of these three, in order to avoid a possible extension of the dispute to the 'coalies' and the tugboatmen, etc. (Purfleet steamers are bunkered from lighters). As in the case of the Head Line, the Secretary specifically drew the attention of the Anglo-American Oil Company to the nature of the complaints, and also sent a written request, following upon a telephone message, by a special messenger for the purpose of saving time. It should be remembered that the bunkers would all be aboard by Tuesday, and this was written on Monday. The Secretary was not very much surprised, however, to receive a reply asking him "what exactly the complaints are, and on whose behalf they are made". The reply was strangely in keeping with the replies received from the Head Line Company. The inference is that both these replies received inspiration from the same source."

We are writing these words in the hope that they will be read by all those responsible for the guidance and control of the Transport Workers in all our seaports. On the face of it, it seems that the one course of action was to call off the men who were working on this ship. If the Company are asking for a fight, what earthly use is it to fight with a portion of your men, leaving all the others to render service to your enemy? This Company has made an open attack on all their employees who are members of the Seamen's Union. At the same time the cargo of oil was being pumped into reservoirs ashore by Trade Union engineers, the men employed ashore are members of an affiliated Union in the Federation, the ship is bunkered by members of an affiliated Union, the tugboats and lighters are staffed by members of an affiliated Union, and still we are powerless.

We are not so fatuous as to suggest that continuous warfare shall be waged by general strikes whenever a member considers he has a grievance, or whenever an official encounters a difficulty, but we feel that we are drifting back to the position we were in prior to 1911. A Federation with 29 Unions as its constituents, but with no ties more binding than the payment of 3d. per member per year, will not, and cannot, meet the requirements of modern industry. We are responsible to a quarter of a million men, and the existing methods are utterly incapable of protecting them from the insidious attacks of the employers. The organization that is afraid of making a massed attack will experience a series of isolated disasters. The workers' organization secures respect and consideration in proportion to the extent to which it can hamper and embarrass the employers against whom it is pitted.

When co-operation is sought from one Union by another, the men involved say – Consult an official. The official says "Get the consent of my E.C.". The Executive officers say – "Communicate with the Transport Workers' Federation." The Federation waits on the decision of its own Executive, and by this inconsequent fiddling of time and opportunity, a thousand Romes would have burned to extinction.

The employers move, strike, move, and strike again with the rapidity of a serpent, while we are turning about and contorting with the facility of an alligator. We have at once to determine whether the future is to mean for us efficiency, aptitude, capacity and life, or muddle, incompetence, decay and death.

Just what is the real remedy for this state of matters, it would be hard to say. But it is at least certain that the organizations I have been speaking of have not discovered the true methods of working-class organizations. They may be on the road to discovering it; they may also be on the road to foisting upon the working class a form of organization which will make our last state infinitely worse than our first. It is the old story of adopting the letter but rejecting the spirit. The letter of industrial concentration is now accepted by all trade union officials, but the spirit of working-class solidarity is woefully absent. Each union and each branch of each union desires above all things to show a good balance sheet, and that that might be done every nerve is strained to keep their members at work, and in a condition to pay subscriptions. Hence the pitiful dodges to avoid taking sympathetic action in support of other unions, and hence also the constant victories of the master class upon the industrial field.

I have often thought that we of the working class are too slow, or too loath, to take advantage of the experience of our rulers. Perhaps if upon all questions of industrial or other war we followed more closely after them we would be able to fight them more successfully. Here is one suggestion I make on those lines. I am not welded to it, but I would like to see it discussed:

In the modern State the capitalist class has evolved for its own purposes of offence what it calls a Cabinet. This Cabinet controls its fighting forces, which must obey it implicitly. If the Cabinet thinks the time and opportunity is ripe for war, it declares war at the most favourable moment, and explains its reasons in Parliament afterwards.

Can we trust any of our members with such a weapon as the capitalist class trusts theirs? I think so. Can we not evolve a system of organization which will leave to the unions the full local administration, but invest in a Cabinet the power to call out the members of any union when such action is desirable, and explain their reasons for it afterwards? Such a Cabinet might have the right to call upon all affiliated unions to reimburse the union whose members were called out in support of another, but such unions so supported would be under the necessity of obeying instantly the call of the Cabinet, or whatever might be the name of the board invested with the powers indicated.

Out of such an arrangement the way would be opened for a more thorough organization of the working class upon the lines of real Industrial Unionism. At present we are too much afraid of each other. Whatever be our form of organization, the spirit of sectionalism still rules and curses our class.

A Continental Revolution

(August 1914)

The outbreak of war on the continent of Europe makes it impossible this week to write to *Forward* upon any other question. I have no doubt that to most of my readers Ireland has ere now ceased to be, in colloquial phraseology, the most important place on the map, and that their thoughts are turning gravely to a consideration of the position of the European socialist movement in the face of this crisis.

Judging by developments up to the time of writing, such considerations must fall far short of affording satisfying reflections to the socialist thinker. For, what is the position of the socialist movement in Europe to-day? Summed up briefly it is as follows:

For a generation at least the socialist movement in all the countries now involved has progressed by leaps and bounds, and more satisfactory still, by steady and continuous increase and development.

The number of votes recorded for socialist candidates has increased at a phenomenally rapid rate, the number of socialist representatives in all legislative chambers has become more and more of a disturbing factor in the calculations of governments. Newspapers, magazines, pamphlets and literature of all kinds teaching socialist ideas have been and are daily distributed by the million amongst the masses; every army and navy in Europe has seen a constantly increasing proportion of socialists amongst its soldiers and sailors, and the industrial organisations of the working class have more and more perfected their grasp over the economic machinery of society, and more and more moved responsive to the socialist conception of their duties. Along with this, hatred of militarism has spread through every rank of society, making everywhere its recruits, and raising an aversion to war even amongst those who in other things accepted the capitalist order of things. Anti-militarist societies and anti-militarist campaigns of socialist societies and parties, and anti-militarist resolutions of socialist and international trade union conferences have become part of the order of the day and are no longer phenomena to be wondered at. The whole working class movement stands committed to war upon war – stands so committed at the very height of its strength and influence.

And now, like the proverbial bolt from the blue, war is upon us, and war between the most important, because the most socialist, nations of the earth. And we are helpless!

What then becomes of all our resolutions; all our protests of fraternisation; all our threats of general strikes; all our carefully-built machinery of internationalism; all our hopes for the future? Were they all as sound and fury, signifying nothing? When the German artilleryman, a socialist serving in the German army of invasion, sends a shell into the ranks of the French army, blowing off their heads; tearing out their bowels, and mangling the limbs of dozens of socialist comrades in that force, will the fact that he, before leaving for the front 'demonstrated' against the war be of any value to the widows and orphans made by the shell he sent upon its mission of murder? Or, when the French rifleman pours his murderous rifle fire into the ranks of the German line of attack, will he be able to derive any comfort from the probability that his bullets are murdering or maiming comrades who last year joined in thundering 'hochs' and cheers of greeting to the eloquent Jaurès, when in Berlin he pleaded for international solidarity? When the socialist pressed into the army of the Austrian Kaiser, sticks a long, cruel bayonet-knife into the stomach of the socialist conscript in the army of the Russian Czar, and gives it a twist so that when pulled out it will pull the entrails out along with it, will the terrible act lose any of its fiendish cruelty by the fact of their common theoretical adhesion to an anti-war propaganda in times of peace? When the socialist soldier from the Baltic provinces of Russia is sent forward into Prussian Poland to bombard towns and villages until a red trail of blood and fire covers the homes of the unwilling Polish subjects of Prussia, as he gazes upon the corpses of those he has slaughtered and the homes he has destroyed, will he in his turn be comforted by the thought that the Czar whom he serves sent other soldiers a few years ago to carry the same devastation and murder into his own home by the Baltic Sea?

But why go on? It is not as clear as the fact of life itself that no insurrection of the working class; no general strike; no general uprising of the forces of Labour in Europe, could possibly carry with it, or entail a greater slaughter of socialists, than will their participation as soldiers in the campaigns of the armies of their respective countries? Every shell which explodes in the midst of a German battalion will slaughter some socialists; every Austrian cavalry charge will leave the gashed and hacked bodies of Serbian or Russian socialists squirming and twisting in agony upon the ground; every Russian, Austrian, or German ship sent to the bottom or blown sky-high will mean sorrow and mourning in the homes of some socialist comrades of ours. If these men must die, would it not be better to die in their own country fighting for freedom for their class, and for the abolition of war, than to go forth to strange countries and die slaughtering and slaughtered by their brothers that tyrants and profiteers might live?

Civilisation is being destroyed before our eyes; the results of generations of propaganda and patient heroic plodding and self-sacrifice are being blown into annihilation from a hundred cannon mouths; thousands of comrades with whose souls we have lived in fraternal communion are about to be done to death; they whose one hope it was to be spared to cooperate in building the perfect society of the future are being driven to fratricidal slaughter in shambles where that hope will be buried under a sea of blood.

I am not writing in captious criticism of my continental comrades. We know too little about what is happening on the continent, and events have moved too quickly for any of us to be in a position to criticise at all. But believing as I do that any action would be justified which would put a stop to this colossal crime now being perpetrated, I feel compelled to express the hope that ere long we may read of the paralysing of the internal transport service on the continent, even should the act of paralysing necessitate the erection of socialist barricades and acts of rioting by socialist soldiers and sailors, as happened in Russia in 1905. Even an unsuccessful attempt at social revolution by force of arms, following the paralysis of the economic life of militarism, would be less disastrous to the socialist cause than the act of socialists allowing themselves to be used in the slaughter of their brothers in the cause.

A great continental uprising of the working class would stop the war; a universal protest at public meetings will not save a single life from being wantonly slaughtered.

I make no war upon patriotism; never have done. But against the patriotism of capitalism – the patriotism which makes the interest of the capitalist class the supreme test of duty and right – I place the patriotism of the working class, the patriotism which judges every public act by its effect upon the fortunes of those who toil. That which is good for the working class I esteem patriotic, but that party or movement is the most perfect embodiment of patriotism which most successfully works for the conquest by the working class of the control of the destinies of the land wherein they labour.

To me, therefore, the socialist of another country is a fellow-patriot, as the capitalist of my own country is a natural enemy. I regard each nation as the possessor of a definite contribution to the common stock of civilisation, and I regard the capitalist class of each nation as being the logical and natural enemy of the national culture which constitutes that definite contribution.

Therefore, the stronger I am in my affection for national tradition, literature, language, and sympathies, the more firmly rooted I am in my opposition to that capitalist class which in its soulless lust for power and gold would bray the nations as in a mortar.

Reasoning from such premises, therefore, this war appears to me as the most fearful crime of the centuries. In it the working class are to be sacrificed that a small clique of rulers and armament makers may sate their lust for power and their greed for wealth. Nations are to be obliterated, progress stopped, and international hatreds erected into deities to be worshipped.

A Martyr For Conscience Sake

(August 1914)

As I am writing this the news appears in the press that our comrade, Dr. Karl Liebknecht, has been shot in Germany for refusing to accept military service in the war. The news is unconfirmed, and will, I trust, be found later to be untrue, but I propose to take it this week as a text for my article.

Supposing, then, that it was true, what would be the socialist attitude toward the martyrdom of our beloved comrade? There can be little hesitation in avowing that all socialists would endorse his act, and look upon his death as a martyrdom for our cause. And yet if his attitude was correct, what can be said of the attitude of all those socialists who have gone to the front, and still more of all those socialists who from press and platform are urging that nothing should be done now that might disturb the harmony that ought to exist at home, or spoil the wonderful solidarity of the nation in this great crisis?

As far as I can understand these latter, their argument seems to be that they did their whole duty when they protested against the war, but that now that war has been declared it is right that they also should arm in defence of their common country, and act in all things along with their fellow subjects – those same fellow subjects whose senseless clamour brought on this awful outburst of murder. We are told, for instance, that the same policy is being pursued by all socialist parties. That the French socialists protested against the war – and then went to the front, headed by Gustave Hervé, the great anti-militarist; the German socialists protested against the war – and then, in the Reichstag, unanimously voted 250 millions to carry it on; the Austrians issued a manifesto against the war – and are now on the frontier doing great deeds of heroism against the foreign enemy; and the Russians erected barricades in the streets of St. Petersburg against the cossacks, but immediately war was declared went off to the front arm in arm with their cossack brothers. And so on. Now, if all this is true, what does it mean? It means that the socialist parties of the various countries mutually cancel each other, and that as a consequence socialism ceases to exist as a world force, and drops out of history in the greatest crisis of the history of the world, in the very moment when courageous action will most influence history.

We know that not more than a score of men in the various Cabinets of the world have brought about this war, that no European people was consulted upon the question, that preparations for it have been going on for years, and that all the alleged 'reasons' for it are so many afterthoughts invented to hide from us the fact that the intrigues and schemes of our rulers had brought the world to this pass. All socialists are agreed upon this. Being so agreed, are we now to forget it all: to forget all our ideas of human brotherhood, and because some twenty highly-placed criminals say our country requires us to slaughter our brothers beyond the seas or the frontiers, are we bound to accept their statement, and proceed to slaughter our comrades abroad at the dictate of our enemies at home. The idea outrages my every sense of justice and fraternity. I may be only a voice crying in the wilderness, a crank amongst a community of the wise, but whoever I be, I must, in deference to my own self-respect, and to the sanctity of my own soul, protest against the doctrine that any decree of theirs of national honour can excuse a socialist who serves in a war which he has denounced as a needless war, can absolve from the guilt of murder any socialist who at the dictate of a capitalist Government draws the trigger of a rifle upon or sends a shot from a gun into the breasts of people with whom he has no quarrel, and who are his fellow labourers in the useful work of civilisation.

We have for years informed the world that we were in revolt against the iniquities of modern civilisation, but now we hear socialists informing us that it is our duty to become accomplices of the rulers of modern civilisation in the greatest of all iniquities, the slaughter of man by his fellow man. And that as long as we make our formal protest we have done our whole duty, and can cheerfully proceed to take life, burn peaceful homes, and lay waste fields smiling with food !

Our comrade, Dr. Liebknecht, if he has died rather than admit this new doctrine, has died the happiest death that man can die, has put to eternal shame the thousands of 'comrades' in every European land, who, with the cant of brotherhood upon their lips, have gone forth in the armies of the capitalist rulers – murdering and to murder. The old veteran leader of German social democracy, his father, Wilhelm Liebknecht, said in one of his pamphlets:

"The working class of the world has but one enemy, the capitalist class of the world, those of their own country at the head of the list."

Well and truly has the son lived up to the truly revolutionary doctrine of the father: lived and died for its eternal truth and wisdom.

Now we are hearing a new excuse for the complicity of socialists in this war. It is that this war will be the last war, its horrors will be so great that humanity will refuse to allow another.

The homely Irish proverb has it that "far off cows have long horns," or that "far away hills are always green." It must have been in some such spirit that this latest argument was evolved. For what can happen in the future that is not more applicable now! In the future this militarist spirit will probably be in the ascendant, new national prejudices will have been born, new international hatreds called forth. There will be memories of recent defeats to wipe out, fresh frontiers to conserve or to obliterate, and the military caste will have acquired an ascendancy over the popular imagination because the large numbers of the various armies will have given rise to widespread solicitude for their welfare and consequent hopes for their success. If you have friends or relatives whom you dearly love serving in the army, you cannot help wishing for the success of that army, and the defeat of its immediate opponents, and from such a state of feeling to the most intense jingoism is but a small and easy transition. The large armies of today draw upon the whole population, all are interested in the fate of their friends or relatives, and we may all be sure that the lying press can be depended upon to convert solicitude for our friends into passionate hatred for those whom war makes their opponents.

No; we cannot draw upon the future for a draft to pay our present duties. There is no moratorium to postpone the payment of the debt the socialists owe to the cause; it can only be paid now. Paid it may be in martyrdom, but a few hundred such martyrdoms would be but a small price to pay to avert the slaughter of hundreds of thousands. If our German comrade, Liebknecht, has paid the price, perhaps the others may yet nerve themselves for that sacrifice. On what conception of national honour can we blame them, before what fetish of national dignity can we prostrate ourselves in abasement to atone for their act?

The war of a subject nation for independence, for the right to live out its own life in its own way may and can be justified as holy and righteous; the war of a subject class to free itself from the debasing conditions of economic and political slavery should at all times choose its own weapons, and hold and esteem all as sacred instruments of righteousness. But the war of nation against nation in the interest of royal freebooters and cosmopolitan thieves is a thing accursed.

All hail, then, to our continental comrade, who, in a world of imperial and financial brigands and cowardly trimmers and compromisers showed mankind that men still know how to die for the holiest of all causes – the sanctity of the human soul, the practical brotherhood of the human race!

The War Upon The German Nation

(August 1914)

Now that the first drunkenness of the war fever is over, and the contending forces are locked in deadly combat upon the battlefield, we may expect that the sobering effect of the reports from the front will help to restore greater sanity to the minds of the people. There are thousands of Irish homes today from which, deluded by the foolish declaration of Mr. Redmond that Ireland was as one with the Empire in this struggle, and the still more foolish and criminal war whoops of the official Home Rule press, there went forth sons and fathers to recruit the armies of England. If to those thousands of Irish homes from which the call of Mr. Redmond drew forth young Irishmen we add the tens of thousands of homes from which reservists were drawn, we have a vast number of Irish homes in which from this day forward gibbering fear and heartbreaking anxiety will be constantly present – forever present at the fireside, unbidden guests at the table, loathsome spectres in the darkness grinning from the pillows and the coverlet.

Each day some one of these homes, some days thousands of these homes will be stricken from the field of battle, and news will come home that this young son or that loving father has met his doom, and out there under a foreign sky the mangled remains, twisted, blown and gashed by inconceivable wounds will lie, each of them in all their ghastly horror crying out to Heaven for vengeance upon the political tricksters who lured them to their fate.

Poor and hunger-harassed as are the members of the Irish Transport & General Workers' Union, is there one of them who today has not a happier position and a clearer conscience than the so-called leaders of the Irish race, who are responsible for deluding into enlisting to fight England's battles the thousands of Irish youths whose corpses will ere many months be manuring the soil of a foreign country, or whose mangled bodies will be contemptuously tossed home to starve - a burden and a horror to all their kith and kin?

Read this report from the *Daily News and Leader* of the 25th inst. of the statement of an Alsatian peasant who saw some of the fighting in Alsace. He says:

"The effects of artillery fire are terrific. The shells burst, and where you formerly saw a heap of soldiers you then see a heap of corpses or a number of figures writhing on the ground, torn and mutilated by the exploded fragments."

And when you have read that then think of the many thousands of our boys – for God help us and them, they are still our brave Irish boys though deluded into fighting for the oppressor – around whom such shells will be falling by day and by night for many a long month to come. Think of them, and think also of the multitude of brave German boys who never did any harm to them or to us, but who rather loved us and our land, and our tongue and our ancient literature, and consider that those boys of ours will be busy sending shot and shell and rifle ball into their midst, murdering and mangling German lives and limbs, widowing humble German women orphaning helpless German children.

Such reflections will perhaps open the way for the more sane frame of mind I spoke of at the beginning of this article. To help in clarifying the thought of our people that such sanity may be fruitful in greater national as well as individual wisdom, permit me, then, to present a few facts to those whose attitude upon the war has been so far determined by the criminal jingoism of the daily press. I wish to try and trace the real origin of this war upon the German nation, for despite all the truculent shouts of a venal press and conscienceless politicians, this war is not a war upon German militarism, but upon the industrial activity of the German nation.

If the reader was even slightly acquainted with the history of industry in Europe he would know that as a result of the discovery of steam as a motive power, and the consequent development of machine industry depending upon coal, Great Britain towards the close of the eighteenth century began to dominate the commercial life of the world. Her large coal supply helped her to this at a time when the coal supply of other countries had not yet been discovered or exploited. Added to this was the fact that the ruling class of England by a judicious mixing in European struggles, by a dexterous system of alliances and a thoroughly unscrupulous use of her sea power was able to keep the Continent continually embroiled in war whilst her own shores were safe. Whilst the cities and towns of other countries were constantly the prey of rival armies, their social life crushed under the cannon wheels of contending forces, and their brightest young men compelled to give to warfare the intellect that might have enriched their countries by industrial achievements, England was able peacefully to build up her industries, to spread her wings of commerce, and to become the purveyor-general of manufactured goods to the civilised and uncivilised nations of the world. In her own pet phrase she was 'the workshop of the world,' and other nations were but as so many agricultural consumers of the products of England's factories and workshops.

Obviously such a state of matters was grossly artificial and unnatural. It could not be supposed by reasonable men that the civilised nations would be content to remain for ever in such a condition of tutelage or dependence. Rather was it certain that self-respecting nations would begin to realise that the industrial overlordship by England of Europe meant the continued dependence of Europe upon England – a most humiliating condition of affairs.

So other nations began quietly to challenge the unquestioned supremacy of England in the markets. They began first to produce for themselves what they had hitherto relied upon England to produce for them, and passed on from that to enter into competition with English goods in the markets of the world. Foremost and most successful European nation in this endeavour to escape from thraldom of dependence upon England's manufactures stands the German nation. To this contest in the industrial world it brought all the resources of science and systematised effort. Early learning that an uneducated people is necessarily an inferior people, the German nation attacked the work of educating its children with such success that it is now universally admitted that the Germans are the best educated people in Europe. Basing its industrial effort upon an educated working class, it accomplished in the workshop results that this half-educated working-class of England could only wonder at. That English working class trained to a slavish subservience to rule-of-thumb methods, and under managers wedded to traditional processes saw themselves gradually outclassed by a new rival in whose service were enrolled the most learned scientists co-operating with the most educated workers in mastering each new problem as it arose, and unhampered by old traditions, old processes or old equipment. In this fruitful marriage of science and industry the Germans were pioneers, and if it seemed that in starting both they became unduly handicapped it was soon realised that if they had much to learn they had at least nothing to unlearn, whereas the British remained hampered at every step by the accumulated and obsolete survivals of past industrial traditions.

Despite the long hold that England has upon industry, despite her pre-emption of the market, despite the influence of her far-flung empire, German competition became more and more a menace to England's industrial supremacy; more and more German goods took the place of English. Some few years ago the cry of 'Protection' was raised in England in the hopes that English trade would be thus saved by a heavy customs duty against imported commodities. But it was soon realised that as England was chiefly an exporting country a tax upon imported goods would not save her industrial supremacy. From the moment that realisation entered into the minds of the British capitalist we may date the inception of this war.

It was determined that since Germany could not be beaten in fair competition industrially, it must be beaten unfairly by organising a military and naval conspiracy against her. British methods and British capitalism might be inferior to German methods and German capitalism; German scientists aided by German workers might be superior to British workers and tardy British science, but the British fleet was still superior to the German in point of numbers and weight of artillery. Hence it was felt that if the German nation could be ringed round with armed foes upon its every frontier until the British fleet could strike at its ocean-going commerce, then German competition would be crushed and the supremacy of England in commerce ensured for another generation. The conception meant calling up the forces of barbaric powers to crush and hinder the development of the peaceful powers of industry. It was a conception worthy of fiends, but what do you expect? You surely do not expect the roses of honour and civilisation to grow on the thorn tree of capitalist competition – and that tree planted in the soil of a British ruling class.

But what about the independence of Belgium? Aye, what about it?

Remember that the war found England thoroughly prepared, Germany totally unprepared. That the British fleet was already mobilised on a scale never attempted in times of peace, and the German fleet was scattered in isolated units all over the seven seas. That all the leading British commanders were at home ready for the emergency, and many German and Austrian officers, such as Slatin Pasha, have not been able to get home yet. Remember all this and realise how it reveals that the whole plan was ready prepared; and hence that the 'Belgium' was a mere subterfuge to hide the determination, to crush in blood the peaceful industrial development of the German nation. Already the British press is chuckling with joy over the capture of German trade. All capitalist journals in England boast that the Hamburg-American Line will lose all its steamers, valued at twenty-millions sterling. You know what that means! It means that a peaceful trade built up by peaceful methods is to be struck out of the hands of its owners by the sword of an armed pirate. You remember the words of John Mitchel descriptive of the British Empire, as "a pirate empire, robbing and plundering upon the high seas."

Understand the game that is afoot, the game that Christian England is playing, and when next you hear apologists for capitalism tell of the wickedness of Socialists in proposing to 'confiscate' property remember the plans of British and Irish capitalists to steal German trade – the fruits of German industry and German science.

Yes, friends, governments in capitalist society are but committees of the rich to manage the affairs of the capitalist class. The British capitalist class have planned this colossal crime in order to ensure its uninterrupted domination of the commerce of the world. To achieve that end it is prepared to bathe a continent in blood, to kill off the flower of the manhood of the three most civilised great nations of

Europe, to place the iron heel of the Russian tyrant upon the throat of all liberty-loving races and peoples from the Baltic to the Black Sea, and to invite the blessing of God upon the spectacle of the savage Cossack ravishing the daughters of a race at the head of Christian civilisation.

Yes, this war is the war of a pirate upon the German nation.

And up from the blood-soaked graves of the Belgian frontiers the spirits of murdered Irish soldiers of England call to Heaven for vengeance upon the Parliamentarian tricksters who seduced them into the armies of the oppressor of their country.

The Friends of Small Nationalities

(September 1914)

The 'war on behalf of small nationalities' is still going merrily on in the newspapers. That great champion of oppressed races, Russia, is pouring her armies into East Prussia land offering freedom and deliverance to all and sundry if they will only take up arms on her behalf – without undue delay. She is to be the judge after the war as to whether they did or did not delay unduly.

The Russian Socialists have issued a strong manifesto denouncing the war, and pouring contempt upon the professions of the Czar in favour of oppressed races, pointing out his suppression of the liberties of Finland, his continued martyrdom of Poland, his atrocious tortures and massacres in the Baltic provinces, and his withdrawal of the recently granted parliamentary liberties of Russia. And to that again add the fact that the Polish Nationalists have warned the Poles against putting any faith in a man who has proven himself incapable of keeping his solemnly pledged faith with his own people, and you will begin to get a saner view of the great game that is being played than you can ever acquire from the lying press of Ireland and England.

Of course, that should not blind you to the splendid stand which the British Government, we are assured, is making against German outrages and brutality and in favour of small nationalities. The

Russian Government is admitted by every publicist in England to be a foul blot upon civilisation. It was but the other day that when the Russian Duma was suppressed by force and many of its elected representatives imprisoned and exiled, an English Cabinet Minister defiantly declared in public, in spite of international courtesies:

"The Duma is dead! Long live the Duma!"

But all that is forgotten now, and the Russian Government and the British Government stand solidly together in favour of small nationalities everywhere except in countries now under Russian and British rule.

Yes, I seem to remember a small country called Egypt, a country that through ages of servitude evolved to a conception of national freedom, and under leaders of its own choosing essayed to make that conception a reality. And I think I remember how this British friend of small nationalities bombarded its chief seaport, invaded and laid waste its territory, slaughtered its armies, imprisoned its citizens, led its chosen leaders away in chains, and reduced the new-born Egyptian nation into a conquered, servile British province.

And I think I remember how, having murdered this new-born soul of nationality amongst the Egyptian people, it signalised its victory by the ruthless hanging at Denshawai of a few helpless peasants who dared to think their pigeons were not made for the sport of British officers.

Also, if my memory is not playing me strange tricks, I remember reading of a large number of small nationalities in India, whose evolution towards a more perfect civilisation in harmony with the genius of their race, was ruthlessly crushed in blood, whose lands were stolen, whose education was blighted, whose women were left to the brutal lusts of the degenerate soldiery of the British Raj.

Over my vision comes also grim remembrances of two infant and I look on the map in vain for them today. I remember that the friend of small nationalities waged war upon them – a war of insolent aggression at the instance of financial bloodsuckers. Britain sent her troops to subjugate them, to wipe them off the map; and although they resisted until the veldt ran red with British and Boer blood, the end of the war saw two small nationalities less in the world.

When I read the attempts of the prize Irish press to work up feeling against the Germans by talk of German outrages at the front, I wonder if those who swallow such yarns ever remember the facts about the exploits of the British generals in South Africa. When we are told of the horrors of Louvain, when the only damage that was done was the result of civilians firing upon German troops from buildings which those troops had in consequence to attack, I remember that in South Africa Lord Roberts issued an order that whenever there was an attack upon the railways in his line of communication every Boer house and farmstead within a radius of ten square miles had to be destroyed.

When I hear of the unavoidable killing of civilians in a line of battle 100 miles long in a densely populated country, being of, as it were, part of the German plan of campaign, I remember how the British swept up the whole non-combatant Boer population into concentration camps, and kept it there until the little children died in thousands of fever and cholera; so that the final argument in causing the Boers to make peace was the fear that at the rate of infant mortality in those concentration camps there would be no new generation left to inherit the republic for which their elders were fighting.

This vicious and rebellious memory of mine will also recur to the recent attempt of Persia to form a constitutional government, and it recalls how, when that ancient nation shook off the fetters of its ancient despotism, and set to work to elaborate the laws and forms in the spirit of a modern civilised representative state, Russia, which in solemn treaty with England had guaranteed its independence, at once invaded it, and slaughtering all its patriots, pillaging its towns and villages, annexed part of its territories, and made the rest a mere Russian dependency. I remember how Sir Edward Grey, who now gushes over the sanctity of treaties, when appealed to to stand by and make Russia stand by the treaty guaranteeing the independence of Persia, coolly refused to interfere.

Oh, yes, they are great fighters for small nationalities, great upholders of the sanctity of treaties!

And the Irish Home Rule press knows this, knows all these things that a poor workman like myself remembers, knows them all, and is cowardly and guiltily silent, and viciously and fiendishly evil.

Let us hope that all Ireland will not some day have to pay an awful price for the lying attacks of the Home Rule press upon the noble German nation.

Let our readers encourage and actively spread every paper, circular, leaflet or manifesto which in these dark days dares to tell the truth.

Thus our honour may be saved; thus the world may learn that the Home Rule press is but a sewer-pipe for the pouring of English filth upon the shores of Ireland.

The Ballot or the Barricades

(October 1914)

Towards the close of last week the British Government flew a kite in Ireland. Flying a kite when practiced by a Government means getting some person or paper to issue a statement that the Government contemplates taking certain action. If the announcement arouses no hostility of a serious nature the action is forthwith taken. If, on the contrary, the announcement is met with a storm of hostility the Government declares it did not authorise and does not contemplate any such action as was announced, and that it regrets that any such statement should have been made by unauthorised persons. Having flown its kite to learn how the wind blows, the Government then proceeds to do a little more spade work to prepare the ground better for taking the action it has just declared it does not intend to take.

The kite flown last week was the announcement that the Militia Ballot Act was to be enforced in Ireland. As it evoked hostility the Government proceeded to officially repudiate it. The ground was not well prepared, the game was too shy. But nevertheless the iniquitous proposal is only temporarily abandoned. In some form or another conscription is inevitable.

The only thing that can avert conscription is the speedy collapse of the German army – a thing as remote as the conversion of England's rulers to Christian principles. Already a responsible authority, Sir Thomas Barclay, has declared that England will, before the close of the war, have two million men with the colours, an army impossible without conscription. In addition to this we have the fact that the slaughter at the front is almost inconceivable. A great surgeon, Dr. Haden Guest, says, that at present the military sick and wounded in France number half a million. Thus the gaps in the firing line require the presence of a continually increasing army of support to fill them. Where and how are all those soldiers to be got, if not by and through some form of conscription?

The truth about the Germany army is that its position becomes more secure every day. At the beginning of the war the Allies joyfully declared that time was on their side, that every day gained was equal to the winning of a battle, that the Allies could afford to wait and the Germans could not. It is now beginning to penetrate the heads of the military experts of Fleet Street that the boot is on the other leg. The Russians were the great hope of England. Unless the Russians can achieve victory before the closing in of the terrible Russian winter that hope is gone. It will be impossible to maintain in the field the enormous masses of Russian troops, to provision them, to keep them supplied with munitions of war, to handle all the elaborate, cumbrous but necessary machinery of transport and commissariat, whilst the snow king has his grip upon Russian railroads and rivers. Add to this the terrible cost of the maintenance of such an army as Russia requires to face the Germans – the most uneducated nation in Europe to face the most educated, and we see at once that England cannot hope to see Russia win the war for her. She must produce the men herself. Russia is bankrupt. The Czar was only able to crush the Russian Revolution because of the loans from France and England. Now these countries need all their moneys for their own salvation.

Thus on the side of Germany there are fighting the influences of time and of money, of superior equipment, and of wise provision for the future.

Therefore the Militia Ballot Act or some form of conscription will come. Are we, like our rulers, to await the evil day, and then 'muddle through' with ineffective protests? Or are we to make provision beforehand for the fight that will be necessary?

We of the Irish Transport & General Workers' Union, we of the Citizen Army, have our answer ready. We will resist the Militia Ballot

Act, or any form of conscription, and we begin now to prepare our resistance. Upon the Volunteers we urge similar resolves, similar preparations.

Understand what this means. It means a complete overhauling and remodelling of all the training and instruction hitherto given to those corps. It means that the corps shall be taught how to act and fight when acting against an enemy equipped with superior weapons, instead of all teaching being based upon the ideas of British military text books which always presume an equality of weapons, or even a superiority upon the British side. It means that much that has been taught will be worse than useless if acted upon, as such teaching presupposed that the corps receiving instructions were to form part of a regular army in the field, an army properly supported and reinforced by complete arms of the service. The resistance to the Militia Ballot Act must of necessity take the form of insurrectionary warfare, if the resisters are determined to fight in Ireland for Ireland instead of on the Continent for England. Such insurrectionary warfare would be conducted upon lines and under conditions for which text books made no provision.

In short, it means barricades in the streets, guerrilla warfare in the country.

To all who are prepared to face that ordeal rather than shed their blood for the tyrant and exploiter we appeal to join our Citizen Army. We propose to make that force the best equipped mentally in Ireland. We want no parade ground soldiers. We want young men prepared to die for Freedom in Ireland. If the Government proposes to force us to fight against our consciences and our desire we propose to challenge it upon its own ground; and if it wants us it must take us by force.

From this date greater decision and promptitude in action will be enforced in our army though even now it is an example to follow. All those who fell away because we had not rifles enough are requested to enroll at once and take a course in the preliminary training in the new course of instruction on the lines we have indicated.

The rifles will come all right. And there are other modern weapons of warfare.

The Citizen Army Offices at Liberty Hall, Aungier Street, Inchicore, Thomas Street, and elsewhere are open every night for enrollment. We want a new muster of men prepared to face the worst and to take the best if taken it can be.

Rally for Labour

(November 1914)

Signs are not wanting in Ireland to-day that there are strenuous and exciting times before the forces of organised Labour. The fever and excitement of the war is practically over, the talk of certain victory and a short war has disappeared from the conversation of even the most optimistic of the employing class, and everywhere we see that the class that rules and robs us is making preparations to take whatever advantage the war may offer to increase its profits, and increase its power over our lives. Capitalist society is so built that the clash of interests is inevitable; here and there at all times, and all over for a short time, these clashing interests may be forgotten in a wave of patriotism or a frenzy of religious enthusiasm; but such unity never survives for long the constant attrition of the divergent interests of the various classes and individuals. Sooner or later the old war of self-interest resumes its domination, and the conflict inherent in capitalist society with all its ugliness and horror, assumes control and direction of the minds, passions and lives of men and women.

When this war broke out there was in England, and amongst those whose outlook on life is that of England, a fine simulation of the self-abnegation of patriotism. Employers in England told their employees that the firm would make up the wages of each man volunteering to the front, and workers left wives and families to trust to the tender mercies of their masters and their government. They were all out against the 'common enemy,' and all distinctions, rivalries and clashing interests were laid aside. It was fine!

But it was too fine to last. Already the Government has shown its bias against trade unionism, and against the working class. The demand of the Parliamentary Labour Party for £1 per week for soldiers is treated with the contempt earned by its sponsors when they delivered the goods before they stipulated for a price, went recruiting for the army first, and only thought of demanding proper payment for recruits after thousands upon thousands had surrendered their liberty and became food for cannon. All through England and Ireland committees under various names are engaged in procuring the manufacture of goods for the army by voluntary labour, whilst the persons – mainly women and girls – normally employed at the manufacture of those goods are turned out on the streets to starve, or else compelled to seek a livelihood by begging these committees to supply them with work under conditions they would scorn if offered at other times by private employers.

A moratorium suspending payment of large sums has been granted to and is freely availed of by the rich, whilst eviction notices are descending as thick as snowflakes upon the helpless poor, and wives and widows of England's soldiery every day throng the police courts begging for permission to keep together a little longer the household gathered by the loving labours of the 'heroes at the front.' Relief of Distress Committees in their work seem to unite in regarding every applicant as a degraded criminal upon whom every insult can be heaped that class hatred can devise, until poor women resolve to die in their slums rather than have their wretchedness marked by the insulting questions and insinuations of the investigators. In Ireland the demand of organised labour for representation upon such committees is made subordinate to the whims and prejudices of every little mind from Lord Mayor Sherlock down to the toadies whose delight it is to eat dirt that has been trodden on by the feet of Lady Aberdeen.

A consignment of flour is sent here from Canada, and the Government ostentatiously gives the work of discharging it to the lowest collection of blacklegs that has ever disgraced Dublin. A law is on the Statute Book empowering the Corporation of Dublin to feed the children starving at school, and the Corporation mocks the law and the children by appointing on that committee the bitterest enemies of the measure, and a chairman who has made up his mind that it shall never be enforced, whilst the claim of the Dublin Trades Council to be represented is met with a flat refusal, as is also the claim of the Ladies' Committee which for years has fed the children of two of our Dublin schools.

War is ever the enemy of progress. It is only possible when humanity is stifled, when the common interests of the human race are denied. The first blast of the bugles of war is also the requiem note of human brotherhood. It is but a step, and a short step, from exulting in the sufferings of a foreign enemy to contemptuous indifference to the sights and sounds of suffering amongst our own poor in our own streets. The poor of the world would be well advised, upon the declaration of war in any country, as their first steps to peace, to hang the Foreign Minister and Cabinet whose secret diplomacy produced such a result. If each country hanged its own Foreign Minister and Cabinet before setting out to the front, wars would not last long; and if a jingo editor were hanged each week it lasted, the most jingo being the first to hang, not many angry passions would be stirred up to make the work of peaceful understanding difficult.

Wanting such a desirable result the workers must realise now that all the machinery of the State, and all the extra machinery now being set up to aid the State, are being deliberately utilised to accentuate the weakness of the individual worker, to intensify the dependence of his dear ones upon charitable and anti-labour organisations, to concentrate in the hands of the enemies of his class all the new agencies of government as well as the old, and in short, to weaken, discredit and destroy every power that the workers have hitherto built up as weapons for their peaceful social regeneration.

Our trade unions are attacked by every insidious weapon, our standard of life is menaced in a thousand evil ways, a corrupt press calls aloud for the suppression of every Irish journal that refuses to prostitute itself. The time is ripe for a forward move against all those gathering forces of evil, every man and woman who has reaped the advantages which organised Labour has won in the past must now rally to the flag. All jealousies must be forgotten, all rivalries laid aside.

Labour is the only force that can save Labour. Rally then to save Labour from its encircling enemies, and know that in saving Labour you save the most effective force for the redemption of Ireland.

Courts-martial and Revolution

(December 1914)

"The Earl of Halsbury said that in deference to the wishes of the Government he would not press his objections, but he thought the proposal of this Bill was the most unconstitutional thing that had ever happened."

The foregoing sentence is from a report of a debate in the House of Lords on the Defence of the Realm Consolidation Act, on Friday, November 27th. This precious Act gives the military authorities power to arrest civilians and try them by Courts-martial, sets aside all the ordinary safeguards of civil liberty, and empowers these Courtsmartial to inflict the death penalty or any lesser sentence. In other words, and plainer language, it establishes Martial Law as the law of the land, and places the lives and liberties of all in the power of a military unaccustomed to the restraints of civilised courts of justice, and ignorant of the laws of evidence.

A German, a French, an Italian or an Austrian Government would have openly and honourably sought to attain those ends by a declaration of Martial Law; the hypocritical and cowardly gang of assassins who control the Government of the British Empire seek to achieve the same objects by clandestinely and treacherously destroying civil liberties whilst professing a desire to safeguard and protect them. This is but a fitting culmination to all the anti-democratic and liberty-hating diplomacy which brought about this war, and now seeks to destroy every agency which would help to unmask its injurious conspiracy against mankind, or tell the truth about the terrors that accompany it. As a result of this Act there is no longer liberty in Ireland – liberty of speech, liberty of association, liberty of the press, liberty of the subject are all gone. No longer may a man or woman demand to be tried by his or her peers in an open court-room, before the eyes and hearing of his or her fellows. At any time any man or woman may be arrested, day or night, and dragged off in secret, to be tried in secret, and condemned and assassinated in secret by the hired assassins of the British Empire.

Aye, there is no break in the continuity of the methods of British Imperial Rule in Ireland. Dublin Castle is always Dublin Castle, the same at all times, loathsome, lying, hypocritical, murderous.

Of course we have the word of this Government that no death sentences will be carried out until Parliament meets, and of course we all know what the word of the Government is worth. Belgium knows it now, knows that this Government pledged its honour to maintain Belgian neutrality, and then manoeuvred to leave Belgium irrevocably committed to sink or swim with one side in this struggle in which she was supposed to remain neutral. Ireland knows it, knows that the Liberal Government pledged its word to give Home Rule to all Ireland then pledged its word to Carson not to force Home Rule upon all Ireland, pledged its word to place a representative of Labour upon the Commission of Inquiry into the Dublin police outrages, then deliberately breaks its solemn word, and appointed no such representatives; pledged its word to appoint an independent Commission of Inquiry into the Bachelor's Walk massacre, and yet declared in Parliament beforehand that the said Commission would exonerate the uniformed murderers of peaceful citizens. Aye, Ireland knows the value of a Government promise, as our fathers knew it in the past!

But let 'messieurs, the assassins,' beware. There are in Ireland today many scores of thousands of earnest men neither committed to the British Empire nor to the cause of revolution. For the most part these are men who, wearied of the chaos of Irish politics, gave a grudging adhesion to the parliamentary attempt to secure some form of Home Rule as an organised legal expression of Irish nationhood.

Loyalty to the party entrusted with that task has kept these men silent and inactive even whilst that party was betraying their trust, and besmirching their ideals. Always the hope persisted that eventually Home Rule would come, and then these traitors would be punished by an outraged people. But if the British Government once more throws off the mask of constitutionalism and launches its weapons of repression against those who dare to differ from it, if once more it sets in motion its jails, its courtsmartial, its scaffolds, then the last tie that binds those men to the official Home Rule gang will snap. On that day we will see once again all the best and brightest in Ireland definitely arraying itself on the side of revolution, fully realising that freedom and the British Empire cannot co-exist in this country.

The constitutional mask, the simulacrum of civil liberty still paralyses the activities and holds the hand of many a true Irish patriot, as the boasted freedom of contract of the wage-system still hides from many a worker the reality of his slavery. But once let the Government drop that mask, or abandon that presence of civil liberty, and then the result will see such a resurrection of Irish revolutionary spirit such as has not been seen for generations.

A resurrection! Aye, out of the grave of the first Irish man or woman murdered for protesting against Ireland's participation in this thrice-accursed war there will arise anew the spirit of Irish revolution.

"The graves of those murdered for freedom bear seed for freedom Which the winds carry afar and re-sow."

Yes, my lords and gentlemen, our cards are all on the table! If you leave us at liberty we will kill your recruiting, save our poor boys from your slaughter-house, and blast your hopes of Empire. If you strike at, imprison, or kill us, out of our prisons or graves we will still evoke a spirit that will thwart you, and, mayhap, raise a force that will destroy you.

We defy you! Do your worst!

Whether this death sentence upon Irish prisoners of these new Courtsmartial will or will not be carried out will depend, not upon the plighted honour or solemn assurances of Cabinet Ministers already foresworn and discredited even in their own country, nor yet upon any action of the degenerate Irish Members of Parliament who sat still and helped to destroy the constitutional rights of which they prate so loudly; nor yet upon the British Labour Members who, like all apostates, are readiest to stab and destroy all those who remain true to that ideal of democratic freedom they have deserted and dishonoured. No, the question of life and death will depend solely upon the temper of the people of Ireland. If they remain dumb, nerveless, lacking in intrepidity, quivering too mutely in the leash laid upon them by the apostles of 'caution and restraint,' then the blow will fall in increasing severity and ferocity, arrest will follow arrest, blow will follow blow, and sentences will increase in savagery in exact proportion to the tameness of the Irish people, until at last the death penalty will once more strike down those who embody the rebellious people of the Irish race. Oh, it is all well planned. Their fathers in Hell could not have planned it better!

Revolutionary Unionism and War

(March 1915)

Since the war broke out in Europe, and since the socialist forces in the various countries failed so signally to prevent or even delay the outbreak, I have been reading everything in American socialist papers or magazines that came to hand; to see if that failure and the reasons therefor, were properly understood, among my old comrades in the United States.

But either I have not seen the proper publications, or else the dramatic side of the military campaigns has taken too firm a hold upon the imagination of socialist writers to allow them to estimate properly the inner meaning of that debacle of political socialism witnessed in Europe when the bugles of war rang out upon our ears.

I am going then to try, in all calmness, to relate the matter as it appears to us who believe that the signal of war ought also to have been the signal for rebellion, that when the bugles sounded the first note for actual war, their notes should have been taken as the tocsin for social revolution. And I am going to try to explain why such results did not follow such actions. My explanation may not be palatable to some; I hope it will be at least interesting to all.

In the first place let me be perfectly frank with my readers as to my own position, now that that possibility has receded out of sight. As the reader will have gathered from my opening remarks, I believe that the socialist proletariat of Europe in all the belligerent countries ought to have refused to march against their brothers across the frontiers, and that such refusal would have prevented the war and all its horrors even though it might have led to civil war. Such a civil war would not, could not possibly have resulted in such a loss of socialist life as this international war has entailed, and each socialist who fell in such a civil war would have fallen knowing that he was battling for the cause he had worked for in days of peace, and that there was no possibility of the bullet or shell that laid him low having been sent on its murderous way by one to whom he had pledged the 'lifelong love of comrades' in the international army of labour.

But seeing that the socialist movement did not so put the faith of its adherents to the test, seeing that the nations are now locked in this death grapple, and the issue is knit, I do not wish to disguise from anyone my belief that there is no hope of peaceful development for the industrial nations of continental Europe whilst Britain holds the dominance of the sea. The British fleet is a knife held permanently at the throat of Europe; should any nation evince an ability to emerge from the position of a mere customer for British products, and to become a successful competitor of Britain in the markets of the world, that knife is set in operation to cut that throat.

By days and by nights the British Government watches and works to isolate its competitor from the comity of nations, to ring it around with hostile foes. When the time is propitious, the blow is struck, the allies of Britain encompass its rival by land and the fleet of Britain swoops upon its commerce by sea. In one short month the commerce-raiding fleet of Great Britain destroys a trade built up in forty years of slow peaceful industry, as it has just done in the case of Germany.

Examining the history of the foreign relations of Great Britain since the rise of the capitalist class to power in that country, the continuity of this policy becomes obvious and as marvellous as it is obvious.

Neither religion nor race affinity nor diversity of political or social institutions availed to save a competitor of England. The list of commercial rivals or would-be rivals is fairly large, and gives the economic key to the reasons for the great wars of Britain. In that list we find Spain, Holland, France, Denmark and now Germany. Britain must rule the waves, and when the continental nations wished to make at the Hague a law forbidding the capture of merchant vessels during war, Britain refused her assent. Naturally! It is her power to capture merchant ships during war that enables Britain to cut the throat of a commercial rival at her own sweet will.

If she had not that power she would need to depend upon her superiority in technical equipment and efficiency; and the uprise in other countries of industrial enterprises able to challenge and defeat her in this world market has amply demonstrated that she has not that superiority any longer.

The United States and Germany lead in crowding Britain industrially; the former cannot be made a target for the guns of militarist continental Europe, therefore escapes for the time being as Britain never fights a white power single-handed. But Germany is caught within the net and has to suffer for her industrial achievements.

The right to capture merchant ships for which Britain stood out against the public opinion of all Europe is thus seen to be the trump card of Britain against the industrial development of the world outside her shores – against that complete freedom of the seas by which alone the nations of the world can develop that industrial status which socialists maintain to be an indispensible condition for socialist triumph.

I have been thus frank with my readers in order that they may perfectly understand my position and the reason therefor, and thus anticipate some of the insinuations that are sure to be levelled against me as one who sympathises neither with the anti-German hysteria of such comrades as Professor George D. Herron nor with the suddenly developed belief in the good faith of Czars shown by Prince Peter Kropotkin.

I believe the war could have been prevented by the socialists; as it was not prevented and as the issues are knit, I want to see England beaten so thoroughly that the commerce of the seas will henceforth be free to all nations – to the smallest equally with the greatest.

But how could this war have been prevented, which is another way of saying how and why did the socialist movement fail to prevent it?

Socialism and the Irish Rebellion

The full answer to that question can only be grasped by those who are familiar with the propaganda that from 1905 onwards has been known as 'industrialist' in the United States and, though not so accurately, has been called 'syndicalist' in Europe.

The essence of that propaganda lay in two principles. To take them in the order of their immediate effectiveness these were: First, that labour could only enforce its wishes by organising its strength at the point of production, i.e., the farms, factories, workshops, railways, docks, ships – where the work of the world is carried on, the effectiveness of the political vote depending primarily upon the economic power of the workers organised behind it. Secondly, that the process of organising that economic power would also build the industrial fabric of the socialist republic, build the new society within the old.

It is upon the first of these two principles I wish my readers to concentrate their attention in order to find the answer to the question we are asking.

In all the belligerent countries of western and central Europe the socialist vote was very large; in none of these belligerent countries was there an organised revolutionary industrial organisation directing the socialist vote nor a socialist political party directing a revolutionary industrial organisation.

The socialist voters having cast their ballots were helpless, as voters, until the next election; as workers, they were indeed in control of the forces of production and distribution, and by exercising that control over the transport service could have made the war impossible. But the idea of thus co-ordinating their two spheres of activity had not gained sufficient lodgment to be effective in the emergency.

No socialist party in Europe could say that rather than go to war it would call out the entire transport service of the country and thus prevent mobilisation. No socialist party could say so, because no socialist party could have the slightest reasonable prospect of having such a call obeyed.

The executive committee of the socialist movement was not in control of the labour-force of the men who voted for the socialist representatives in the legislative chambers of Europe, nor were the men in control of the supply of labour-force in control of the socialist representatives. In either case there would have been an organised power immediately available against war. Lacking either, the socialist parties of Europe when they had protested against war, had also fired their last shot against militarism and were left like 'children crying in the night.'

Had the socialist party of France been able to declare that rather than be dragged into war to save the Russian Czar from the revolutionary consequences which would have followed his certain defeat by Germany, they would declare a railway strike, there would have been no war between France and Germany, as the latter country saved from the dread of an attack in the west whilst defending itself in the east could not have coerced its socialist population into consenting to take the offensive against France.

But the French government knows, the German government knows, all cool observers in Europe know, that the socialist and syndicalist organisation of France could not have carried out such a threat even had they made it. Both politically and industrially the revolutionary organisations of France are mere skeleton frameworks, not solid bodies.

Politically large numbers roll together at elections around the faithful few who keep the machinery of the party together; industrially, more or less, large numbers roll together during strikes or lock-outs. But the numbers of either are shifting, uncertain and of shadowy allegiance. From such no revolutionary action of value in face of modern conditions of warfare and state organisation could be expected. And none came.

Hence the pathetic failure of French socialism – the socialist battalion occupying the position of the most tactical importance on the European battlefield. For neither Russia nor Britain could have fought had France held aloof; Russia because of the fear of internal convulsions; Britain, because Britain never fights unless the odds against her foe are overwhelming. And Britain needed the aid of the French fleet.

To sum up then, the failure of European socialism to avert the war is primarily due to the divorce between the industrial and political movements of labour. The socialist voter, as such, is helpless between elections. He requires to organise power to enforce the mandate of the elections and the only power he can so organise is economic power –

the power to stop the wheels of commerce, to control the heart that sends the life blood pulsating through the social organism.

Insurrectionary Warfare

(1915)

Irish Citizen Army HQ: Liberty Hall Commandant: J. Connolly Chief of Staff: M. Mallin

We propose to give under this heading from time to time accounts of such military happenings in the past as may serve to enlighten and instruct our members, in the work they are banded together to perform. A close study of these articles will we hope, be valuable to all those who desire to acquire a knowledge of how brave men and women have at other times and in other place, overcome difficulties and achieved something for a cause held to be sacred. It is not our place to pass verdict on the sacredness or worth of the cause for which they contended: our function is to discuss their achievements from the standpoint of their value to those who desire to see perfected a Citizen Army able to perform whatever duty may be thrust upon it.

We would suggest that these articles be preserved for reference purposes.

Moscow Insurrection of 1905

In the year 1905, the fires of revolution were burning very brightly in Russia. Starting with a parade of unarmed men and women to the palace of the Tsar, the flames of insurrection spread all over the land. The peaceful parades were met with volleys of shrapnel and rifle fire, charged by mounted Cossacks, and cut down remorselessly by cavalry of the line, and in answer to this attack, general strikes broke out all over Russia. From strikes the people proceeded to revolutionary uprisings, soldiers revolted and joined the people in some cases, and in others the sailors of the navy seized the ironclads of the Tsar's fleet and hoisted revolutionary colours. One incident in this outburst was the attempted revolution in Moscow. We take it as our task this week because, in it, the soldiers remained loyal to the Tsar, and therefore it resolved itself into a clean-cut fight between a revolutionary force and a government force. Thus we are able to study the tactics of (a) a regular army in attacking a city defended by barricades, and (b) a revolutionary force holding a city against a regular army.

Fortunately for our task as historians, there was upon the spot an English journalist of unquestioned ability and clearsightedness, as well as of unrivalled experience as a spectator in warfare. This was H.W. Nevinson, the famous war-correspondent. From his book *The Dawn of Russia* as well as from a close intimacy with many refugees who took part in the revolution, this description is built up.

The revolutionists of Moscow had intended to postpone action until a much later date in the hope of securing the co-operation of the peasantry, but the active measures of the government precipitated matters. Whilst the question of "Insurrection" or "No Insurrection yet" was being discussed at a certain house in the city, the troops were quietly surrounding the building and the first intimation of their presence received by the revolutionists was the artillery opening fire on the building at point-blank range. A large number of the leaders were killed or arrested, but next morning the city was in insurrection.

Of the numbers engaged on the side of the revolutionists, there is considerable conflict of testimony. The government estimate, anxious to applaud the performance of the troops, is 15,000. The revolutionary estimate, on the other hand, is only 500. Mr Nevinson states that a careful investigator friendly to the revolutionists, and with every facility for knowing, gave the number as approximately 1,500. The deductions we were able to make from the stories of the refugees aforementioned makes the latter number seem the most probable. The equipment of the revolutionists was miserable in the extreme. Among the 1,500 there was only a total of 80 rifles, and a meagre supply of ammunition for same. The only other weapons were revolvers and automatic pistols, chiefly Brownings. Of these latter a goodly supply seems to have been on hand as at one period of the fighting the revolutionists advertised for volunteers, and named Browning pistols as part of the "pay" for all recruits.

Against this force, so pitifully armed, the government possessed in the city 18,000 seasoned troops, armed with magazine rifles, and a great number of batteries of field artillery.

The actual fighting, which lasted nine days, during which time the government troops made practically no progress, is thus described by the author we have already quoted.

Of the barricades, he says that they were erected everywhere, even the little boys and girls throwing them up in the most out-of-the-way places, so that it was impossible to tell which was a barricade with insurgents to defend it and which was a mock barricade, a circumstance which greatly hindered the progress of the troops, who had always to spend a considerable period in finding out the real nature of the obstruction before they dared to pass it.

The very multitude of these barricades (early next morning I counted one hundred and thirty of them, and I had not seen half) made it difficult to understand the main purpose of all the fighting.

As far as they had any definite plan at all, their idea seems to have been to drive a wedge into the heart of the city, supporting the advance by barricades on each side so as to hamper the approach of troops.

The four arms of the cross roads were blocked with double or even treble barricades about ten yards apart. As far as I could see along the curve of the Sadavoya, on both sides, barricade succeeded barricade, and the whole road was covered with telegraph wire, some of it lying loose, some tied across like netting. The barricades enclosing the centre of the cross roads like a fort were careful constructions of telegraph poles or the iron supports to the overhead wires of electric trams, closely covered over with doors, railings and advertising boards, and lashed together with wire. Here and there a tramcar was built in to give solidity, and on the top of every barricade waved a little red flag.

"Men and women were throwing them (the barricades) up with devoted zeal, sawing telegraph poles, wrenching iron railings from their sockets, and dragging out the planks from builders' yards."

Noteworthy as an illustration of how all things, even popular revolutions, change their character as the conditions change in which they operate, is the fact that no barricade was defended in the style of the earlier French or Belgian revolutions.

Mr Nevinson says:

> But it was not from the barricades themselves that the real opposition came. From first to last no barricade was "fought" in the old sense of the word. The revolutionary methods were far more terrible and effective. By the side-street barricades, and wire entanglements they had rid themselves of the fear of cavalry. By the barricades across the main streets, they had rendered the approach of troops necessarily slow. To the soldiers, the horrible part of the street fighting was that they could never see the real enemy. On coming near a barricade or the entrance to a side street, a few scouts would be advanced a short distance before the guns. As they crept forward, firing as they always did, into the empty barricades in front, they might suddenly find themselves exposed to a terrible revolver fire, at about fifteen paces range, from both sides of the street. It was useless to reply, for there was nothing visible to aim at. All they could do was to fire blindly in almost any direction. Then the revolver fire would suddenly cease, the guns would trundle up and wreck the houses on both sides. Windows fell crashing on the pavement, case-shot burst into the bedrooms, and round-shot made holes through three or four walls. It was bad for furniture, but the revolutionists had long ago escaped through a labyrinth of courts at the back, and were already preparing a similar attack on another street.

The troops did not succeed in overcoming the resistance of the insurgents but the insurrection rather melted away as suddenly as it had taken form. The main reason for this sudden dissolution lay in receipt of discouraging news from St Petersburg from which quarter help had been expected, and was not forthcoming, and in the rumoured advance of a hostile body of peasantry eager to co-operate with the soldiery against the people who were "hindering the sale of agricultural produce in the Moscow market".

Criticism

The action of the soldiery in bringing field-guns, or indeed any kind of artillery, into the close quarters of street fighting was against all the teaching of military science, and would infallibly have resulted in the loss of the guns had it not been for the miserable equipment of the insurgents. Had any body of the latter been armed with a reasonable supply of ammunition the government could only have taken Moscow from the insurgents at the cost of an appalling loss of life.

A regular bombardment of the city would only have been possible if the whole loyalist population had withdrawn outside the insurgent lines, and apart from the social reasons against such an abandonment of their business and property, the moral effect of such a desertion of Moscow would have been of immense military value in strengthening the hands of the insurgents and bringing recruits to their ranks. As the military were thus compelled to fight in the city and against a force so badly equipped, not much fault can be found with their tactics.

Of the insurgents also it must be said that they made splendid use of their material. It was a wise policy not to man the barricades and an equally wise policy not to open fire at long range where the superior weapons of the enemy would have been able with impunity to crush them, but to wait before betraying their whereabouts until the military had come within easy range of their inferior weapons.

Lacking the co-operation of the other Russian cities, and opposed by the ignorant peasantry, the defeat of the insurrection was inevitable, but it succeeded in establishing the fact that even under modern conditions the professional soldier is, in a city, badly handicapped in a fight against really determined civilian revolutionaries.

Insurrection in the Tyrol

In the course of the present war between Italy and the Central States, the Tyrol is likely to come once more into fame as the theatre of military operations. Therefore the story of the insurrection in the

Tyrol in 1809 may be doubly interesting to the reader as illustrating alike the lessons of civilian warfare, and the nature of the people and the country in question.

The Tyrol is in reality a section of the Alpine range of mountains – that section which stretches eastward from the Alps of Switzerland, and interposes between the southern frontier of Germany and the northern frontier of Italy. It is part of the territory of Austria; its inhabitants speak the German language, and for the most part are passionately attached to the Catholic religion. They are described by Alison, the English historian, in terms that read strange to-day in view of the English official attitude to all things German. Alison says: "The inhabitants like all those of German descent, are brave, impetuousus, and honest, tenacious of custom, fearless of danger, addicted to intemperance." The latter clause was in itself not sufficient to make any people remarkable, as at that period heavy drinking was the rule all over Europe, and nowhere worse than in these islands. But the Tyrolese were also well accustomed to the use of arms, and frequent target practice in the militia and trained bands as well as in hunting had made excellent shots of a large proportion of the young men of the country.

After the defeat of Austria in 1805 by Napoleon, the Tyrol was taken from that Empire by the Treaty of Presburg and ceded to Bavaria, the ally of Napoleon. The Tyrolese resented this unceremonious disposal of their country, a resentment that was much increased by the licentious conduct of the French Soldiers sent as garrison into the district. Brooding over their wrongs they planned revolt, and sought and obtained a promise of co-operation from the Austrian Emperor.

In the revolt, alike in its preparation and in its execution, there were three leading figures. These were Andreas Hofer, Spechbacher, and Joseph Haspinger. Hofer, the chief, was an innkeeper, and of great local influence, which he owed alike to his high character and to the opportunities of intercourse given him by his occupation, a more important one before the advent of railroads than now. Spechbacher was a farmer and woodsman, and had been an outlaw and poacher for many years before settling down to married life. Joseph Haspinger was a monk, and from the colour of his beard was familiarly known at Roth-Bart or Redbeard.

It will be observed that none of the three were professional soldiers, yet they individually and collectively defeated the best generals of the French Army – an army that had defeated the professional militarists of all Europe.

The eighth day of April, 1809 was fixed for the rising, and on that date the signal was given by throwing large heaps of sawdust in to the River Inn, which ran all through the mountains, by lighting fires upon the hill tops, and by women and children who carried from house to house little balls of paper on which were written *"es ist zeit"*, "it is time".

At one place, St. Lorenzo, the revolt had been precipitated by the action of the soldiers, whose chiefs, hearing of the project, attempted to seize a bridge which commanded communications between the upper part of the valley and Brunecken. Without waiting for the general signal the peasants in the locality rose to prevent the troops getting the bridge. The Bavarian, General Wrede, with 2,000 men and three guns marched to suppress this revolt, but the peasants hid behind rocks and trees, and taking advantage of every kind of natural cover poured in a destructive fire upon the soldiers. The latter suffered great loss from this fire, but pushed forward, and the peasantry were giving way before the disciplined body when they were reinforced by the advanced guard of an Austrian force coming to help the insurrection. The Bavarians gave way. When they reached the bridge at Laditch the pursuit was so hot that they broke in two, one division going up, the other down, the river. The greater part were taken prisoners at Balsano, amongst the prisoners being one general.

At Sterzing Hofer took charge. Here the peasants were attacked by a large force of soldiers, but they took refuge in thickets and behind rocks and drove off the attacks of the infantry. When the artillery was brought up the nature of the ground compelled the guns to come up in musketry range, and then the peasant marksmen picked off the gunners, after which feat the insurgents rushed in and carried all before them in one impetuous charge. Three hundred and ninety prisoners were taken and 240 killed and wounded.

A column of French under Generals Bisson and Wrede made an attempt to force its way up the Brenner. The peasants fell back before it until it reached the narrow defile of Lueg, where it suffered severely as the insurgents had broken down the bridges and barricaded the roads by heaps of fallen trees. The troops were shot down in heaps as they halted before the barricades and bridges whilst a part of their number laboured to open the way.

Meanwhile another large body of peasants had attacked and taken Innsbruck, the capital of the Tyrol, and when Bisson and Wrede eventually forced their way up the Brenner with the insurgents everywhere harrying on their flanks and rear, picking them off from behind cover, and rushing upon and destroying any party unfortunate enough to get isolated, as they advanced into the open it was only to find the city in possession of the insurgents, and vast masses of armed enemies awaiting them at every point of vantage. After a short fight Bisson, caught between two fires, surrendered with nearly 3,000 men.

Spechbacher took Hall in the Lower Tyrol. A curious evidence of the universality of the insurrection was here given by the circumstance that as none of the men could be spared from the fighting line 400 prisoners had to be marched off under an armed escort of women.

In one week the insurgents had defeated 10,000 regular soldiers experienced in a dozen campaigns and taken 6,000 prisoners.

In a battle at Innsbruck on May 28th-29th the women and children took part, carrying food and water and ammunition. When the insurgents had expended all their lead the women and children collected the bullets fired by the enemy and brought them to the men to fire back at the soldiers. Amongst the number Spechbacher's son, ten years of age, was as active as any, and more daring than most.

After the total defeat of the Austrians and the capture of Vienna by Napoleon, the city of Innsbruck was retaken by a French army of 30,000 men. Hofer was summoned by the French General to appear at Innsbruck. He replied stating that he "would come but it would be attended by 10,000 sharpshooters."

At first the peasantry had been so discouraged by their abandonment by the Austrians that a great number of them had gone to their homes, but at the earnest solicitation of their leaders they again rallied, and hostilities re-opened on August 4th.

A column of French and Bavarians were crossing the bridge at Laditch where the high road from Balsano to the capital crosses the river Eisach. The Tyrolese under Haspinger occupied the overhanging woods, and when the troops were well in the defile they rained bullets and rocks upon them without showing themselves. Men were falling at every step, and the crushing rocks tore lanes through the ranks. The soldiers pressed on until the narrowest point of the defile was reached when a sudden silence fell upon the mountain side. Awestruck, the column involuntarily halted, and amid the silence a voice rang out –"Shall I? Shall I? Stephen." and another answered – "Not yet, not yet."

Recovering, the troops resumed their march in silence and apprehension, and then as they wound deeper into the path the second voice again rang out –

"Now, in the name of the Father, Son and Holy Ghost, cut loose." And at the word, a hinge platform of tree trunks, upon which tons of rocks had been collected, was suddenly cut loose, and the whole mass descended like an avalanche upon the soldiery, sweeping whole companies away and leaving a trail of mangled bodies behind it. Despite this terrible catastrophe the column pushed its way on towards the bridge, only to find it in flames, and a raging torrent barring their further progress. They retreated to their starting point harassed all the way by the invisible enemy and with a loss of 1,200 men.

On August 10th Marshal Lefebre, with 20,000 men, attempted to force a passage through and over the Brenner. He was attacked everywhere by small bodies, his progress checked, and his way barred by every obstacle that nature could supply, or ingenuity suggest, and eventually driven back, losing 25 cannon and the whole ammunition of his army.

On August 12th, with 23,000 foot, 2,000 horse, and 40 cannon, he was attacked at Innsbruck by the three insurgent leaders and defeated. Hofer had kept his promise to come to Innsbruck "with 10,000 sharpshooters". The French lost 6,000 killed, wounded and prisoners.

This was the last notable success of the insurgents. The French having made peace with Austria, and having no other war on hand, were able to concentrate upon the Tyrol a force sufficient to make further resistance impossible. The insurgents returned to their homes, and resistance was abandoned.

Remarks

The nature of the country lent itself to the mode of fighting of the insurgents. But their own genius also counted for much. They used every kind of cover, seldom exposed themselves, and at all times took care not to let bravery degenerate into rashness.

Every effort was made to tempt artillery into close range, the insurgents lying as quiet as possible until such time as their muskets could be brought into play upon the artillery men. To the same end positions were taken up which seemed often to be in direct contravention of military science, since they seemed to abandon every chance of a clear field of fire in front, and enabled the enemy to approach closely without coming under fire. But their seeming mistake was based upon sound judgment as the superior weapons of the enemy would have beaten down opposition from a distance, whereas being compelled to come close in before opening fire the regular soldiery lost their chief advantage over the insurgents and were deprived of the advantages conferred by discipline and efficient control by skilled officers.

Revolution in Belgium

After the defeat and final deposition of Napoleon the Allied Sovereigns met at Vienna in 1815 and proceeded to settle Europe. All during the war against Napoleon all the Continental Powers in alliance with the British Empire had loudly declared to the world and to their respective peoples that they were fighting for Liberty, for National rights, and against foreign oppression. But when they met at Vienna the Allies proceeded to ride roughshod over all the things for which they were supposed to be fighting. Nations in many instances were ruthlessly partitioned, as in the case of Italy, or were subjected to new foreign rulers without being consulted in any manner. This latter was the case of Belgium. That country was forcibly placed under the rule of Holland. Belgium could not resist as the whole of Europe, except France, was represented at the Vienna Congress, and the armies of all Europe were at the call of the Powers for the enforcement of the decrees of that Congress. In passing, it may be said that this settlement of Europe by the Allied Powers was so utterly at variance with the will of the people, so flagrant a denial and suppression of all that the Allies had pretended to fight for that it led to revolution, subsequently, in every state in Europe.

Holland in its rule over Belgium was accused by the Belgians of a systematic campaign against every expression and manifestation of Belgian national life. It was alleged that it penalised the native language of Belgium, and gave undue official preference to the Dutch, that it sought to place Dutch officials in all posts to the exclusion of equally well qualified Belgians, that it unduly favoured Dutch industries by legislation and retarded Belgian, and that in every possible way Belgium was treated more as a conquered province than as an Allied State.

These grievances were agitated in many ways, and many efforts were made to obtain remedies without avail. Eventually in 1830, fifteen years after the settlement by the Congress of Vienna revolution broke out in Brussels.

On the 25th of August, 1830, a partially armed mob attacked the house and printing establishment of the chief pro-Dutch paper, the *National*. After wrecking these they obtained more arms by sacking gunsmiths' shops. Then the official residence of the Dutch Minister of Justice, M. van Mannen, was attacked, gutted, and burned to the ground.

On the 26th the troops were called out and fighting took place in the streets. The crowd had got possession of a large amount, of arms and ammunition and successfully withstood the soldiery. Eventually the troops withdrew in a body to the Place Royale, the reason for the withdrawal being thus stated in the English Press of the time that "in street warfare regular troops, who to be effective must act together, fight at a great disadvantage."

The streets of the city were thus left clear to the people, who proceeded to wreak their vengeance upon the houses and offices of the Government officials. The houses of the Public Prosecutor (Procureur du Roi), of the Director of Police, and of the Commandant of the city were sacked, the furniture being taken out, piled up in the street and burned.

Up till this period the middle class Belgians had only looked on passively, but now they organised themselves into a Burgher Guard to defend their property, and took possession of the city partly by force, partly by agreement with the armed workers who up to this time had done all the fighting. Five thousand Burgher Guards were enrolled, the Commandant being one Baron Hoogvorst. All the military posts in the city were occupied by the Guard, the military remaining inactive outside.

A Committee of Public Safety elected by the Burgher Guard issued a Manifesto setting forth the grievances of the Belgian Nation, and instituting reforms. Clause XI of the Manifesto ordered that

"Bread be distributed to all unfortunate workmen to supply their wants until they are able to resume their labour."

On the 20th of August Royal troops marched upon Brussels, but halted outside upon being told that if they attempted to enter they would be resisted, but the Guard would keep order within if the troops remained outside. As yet there had been no talk of separation, but all Royal colours had been torn down, and distinctive Belgian colours hoisted on the buildings, and worn by the armed people.

On the 30th of August the Prince of Orange arrived outside Brussels and sent in word that he was about to enter. He was informed that he could only enter alone or with his own aide-de-camp. He then threatened to storm the city, and the people replied by building barricades in all the leading streets, and occupying the gates in force. Then the Prince issued a proclamation commanding the inhabitants to lay aside their rebellious colours and badges, and that he would enter the city and take over their duties. This was refused, and he then consented to enter the city alone.

A deputation had been sent to the king at the Hague to lay before him the demands of the Belgians. He met the deputation very courteously, as kings always do when in difficulties, promised many reforms, but insisted that his son, the Prince, should enter Brussels at the head of his troops, and that the deputation should confer with the Minister of the Interior. This latter conference took place, and at it the delegates presented a new demand – the separation of Belgium from Holland, and its erection into an independent Kingdom under the same king.

On this point, like Ireland in our day, the country was divided. Antwerp and Ghent petitioned against separation. Tournay, Verviers, Mons and Namur declared for separation, and in each of them the Civic Guard seized the town and proclaimed the revolution. Bruges followed suit. In each of those places, whilst the Civic Guard was hesitating, the working class took the lead and forced the pace, bringing the guard eventually into line.

On the 19th September the working class of Brussels, tired of the hesitation and inaction of the middle class represenatives, took matters in their own hands, rose in rebellion and marched on the Town Hail. There they seized 40 stand of arms. Next day they took possession of the Town Hall, and all the military posts in the city, and were fortunate enough to get possession of a large supply of arms and ammunition. They dissolved the middle class Committee of Public Safety, and established a Provisional Government.

On the 21st September Prince Frederick advanced upon Brussels and ordered that the guard should surrender their posts, all rebel colours should be taken down, all armed strangers expelled, and threatening to hold responsible personally all members of the Committee of Public Safety, of the Council of Officers of Guards, and of the Municipal Administration. But as all these bodies had been dissolved the Proclamation fell rather flat. The people prepared to fight.

Barricades were thrown up in all the streets and at the gates. Pavements were torn up, stones carried to the top of houses in streets through which the troops would have to pass, and every preparation made, the women being specially busy in the preparations. The attack began on the 22nd, the middle class citizens who had been in the Burgher Guard kept carefully to their houses and out of the fighting. The troops made the attack upon six different points, or districts towards which they opened, Flanders, Auderlecht, Lacken, Schaarbeck, Namur, Louvain. The artillery easily broke through the gates and adjoining barricades but as they advanced, obstacle succeeded obstacle, resistance seemed to multiply itself with every step, and the fighting increased in intensity the farther into the city they penetrated. At the Flanders gate the troops swept at first everything before them with their artillery fire. They advanced with great steadiness until they were met by a strong barricade at a curve in the street which prevented the artillery from being brought to bear. Here they were exposed to a deadly fire from behind the barricade, and overwhelmed from above with showers of paving stones, heavy pieces of furniture, hatchets, fire-irons and every species of missile. Beaten back, they were compelled to retreat. At Auderlecht gate the same fate overtook the soldiery, and at Lacken the insurgents compelled a retreat with great loss.

The division which attacked at Schaarbeck gate fought its way in until it reached an open park in which it took refuge from the close quarters and dreadful hostility of the streets. Then it halted afraid to advance further against the streets. The divisions attacking by Namur and Louvain gates also fought their way in for a short distance and then halted, fearful of attempting a further advance.

On the 24th the middle class joined the insurgent working class, and the fighting was renewed. After a long day's contest the troops were unable to advance, although they had made themselves masters of one of the main streets. The insurgents were still in possession, but too badly organised to expel the troops from their foothold in the city.

On the 26th and 27th volunteers from neighbouring towns joined the insurgents, and, encouraged by their aid, the insurgents began to close in on the troops and drive them back. Eventually, believing their position to be hopeless, the soldiery gave up the struggle and withdrew from the city.

The total insurgent loss from the 22nd to the 27th was stated to he 165 killed and 311 wounded.

After the retreat from Brussels the Government had no foothold in Belgium except in its fortresses. The populace rose in the towns, the Belgian regiments declared in favour of the revolution, and one after another the fortresses fell into the hands of the insurgents.

At Ath and Mons the Dutch garrison was made prisoner. At Namur the garrison surrendered the fortress on condition that it was allowed to depart. At Liege 1,100 men, constituting the garrison, made the same arrangement. Ghent held out against the revolution until October 16th, when it also surrendered on like terms to Namur. By the end of October the Belgians were in possession of all the fortresses except Antwerp, Maastricht and Luxemburg.

On the 10th November a National Congress established the Kingdom of Belgium, which was afterwards formally acknowledged by all the powers.

Remarks

The Revolution in Brussels and the successful stand of an insurgent body against regular troops, made such an impression upon Europe that it was long held as an axiom that it was the duty of the officers in command of the army, confronted with such a condition, to refuse to fight in the streets, and content themselves with a regular investment or siege of the city. The official English view has always dissented from this advice.

Two things have to be kept in mind in studying the Brussels Revolution:

First – that, unlike Continental revolutions in general, there were no defections among the troops. It was two nations in conflict. Hence the revolution at Brussels won purely because of its military position and strength.

Second – that the invention of smokeless powder would tend to make such street fighting far more deadly and demoralising to an army which could not see from whence came the shots that decimated the ranks.

Defence of the Alamo

In 1821 Mexico was separated from the kingdom of Spain and entered upon a turbulent and troubled existence of its own. At that time almost all of the territory comprised in the present American State of Texas was an integral part of the Mexican Republic. It was inhabited largely by Mexicans and other persons of Spanish or mixed Spanish and Indian descent. But along with these there were a large number of immigrants from the United States, some of whom had taken up land under the laws of the Mexican Government, whilst others were hunters, trappers, and adventurers. All these latter were rather disinclined to submit to the laws of the Mexicans, especially when the various changes in the Mexican Government made it at times somewhat problematical what these laws were, and still more of a problem to judge how each fresh incumbent in office would administer the laws. Consequently, the uneasiness grew in volume with each accession of strength in the numbers of the immigrants, and each fresh caprice of the rulers. To add to this uneasy situation the designs of the slaveholders in the United States included an extension of slaveholding territory to the South. Unable to extend the slave belt to the North, and menaced by the continual growth of free states in the West, the slaveholders of the United States were anxious to secure fresh territories which could be erected into slave states whose votes could be counted upon against the pressing changes of the increase of liberationist sentiment in the Congress and Senate. Hence the restless immigrants in Texas received secret encouragement from the United States Government, and having real and genuine grievances of their own their restlessness gradually developed into rebellion.

A Mexican Congress in 1835 adopted a new Constitution for the country, one feature of which was the dissolution of all power in a Congress to meet in Mexico City. This was resented in many parts of the country, and in March 1836, a Texan Congress met at Washington, Texas, and declared Texas to be a free and independent Republic. A provisional Government was organised, and Sam Houston was declared Commander-in-Chief. Hostilities commenced immediately.

Fighting took place at several places, notably at San Antonio de Bexar, where the insurgents after five days battle in the street, compelled the garrison to surrender. On hearing of this disaster to his forces, the Mexican President, Santa Anna, crossed the Rio Grande, the river which forms the boundary line between Texas and Mexico, with an army of 10,000 men, and advanced against the insurgents. In the path of their advance lay an old wooden fort known as the Alamo, into which a Texan officer named Travis threw himself with a garrison of 145 men. The Mexican force laid siege to the place, and Travis sent off the following message for reinforcements:

"The enemy have demanded me to surrender at discretion, otherwise the garrison is to be put to the sword. I have answered his summons with a cannon shot. Our flag still floats proudly from the walls. We shall never surrender or retreat. Liberty or death!"

The little Texan force of one hundred and forty five insurgents held out for ten days against the Mexican army of 10,000 men. Again and again the Mexicans attempted to storm the place, and as often they were beaten off. The wounded were propped up by their comrades and kept on fighting until death, the rushes of the regular soldiery with bayonets were beaten off by the Texans with clubbed rifles or met with the quick deadly work of bowie knives, and when at last the building was taken and the Mexicans were victorious it was found that the loss they had sustained was without a parallel in history. Fifteen hundred Mexicans had been killed or ten for every Texan engaged.

No quarter was given or asked. All the defenders were killed, their bodies collected in a heap and burned.

But the defence of the Alamo had enabled the insurgents elsewhere to organise their resistance, and General Samuel Houston with twelve hundred men was by this time in the field and in a position to conduct a regular campaign. Houston pursued a retreating and waiting policy, refusing to be drawn prematurely into a battle, but patiently biding his time and keeping his men together until he had made them into an army.

Eventually on April 19th, 1836, the two armies met at Buffalo Bayou and the Mexicans were defeated with great slaughter, their General and six hundred men being taken prisoners.

This ended the campaign, the independence of Texas being shortly afterwards formally acknowledged.

Remarks

The defence of the Alamo was one of those defeats which are often more valuable to a cause than many loudly trumpeted victories. It gave spirit and bitterness to the Texan forces, and more important still gave time to their comrades elsewhere. Fortunately for their cause also they had in Houston a General who recognised that the act of keeping an insurgent force in the field was in itself so valuable an establishment of the revolutionary position that it gave all the functions and prestige of government. Hence he kept his force in the field without fighting as long as possible, despite the murmurs of his men, and only hazarded an engagement when he considered that his army was made.

Revolution in Paris, 1830

After the deposition of Napoleon by the allied powers the Bourbon family was restored to the throne of France much against the will of the French people. That family at first made some slight concession to the spirit of democracy which the French revolution had aroused in Europe, but gradually as the people advanced in their claims for enfranchisement the royal family and court became more and more reactionary and opposed to reform.

Eventually the Government took steps to suppress the freedom of the press, and four journals active in the reform movement were proceeded against, their editors sentenced to prison and to pay heavy fines. The Chamber of Deputies took sides against the king, and presented to him an address in favour of reform. He dissolved the Chamber and ordered a general election.

When the election was over it was found that, despite the restricted suffrage and persistent government terrorism, the Reform party out of a total Chamber of 428 members had returned 270, whilst the ministry had only returned 145.

As his answer to the elections the king on the 25th July, 1830, issued a decree destroying at one swoop all the liberties of his subjects.

The new Chamber of Deputies was dissolved before it had even met.

Liberty of the press was suspended. Writings published in violation of the regulations were to be seized, and types and presses used in printing them to be taken into custody, or rendered unfit for their purposes.

The method of election was altered so as to put it completely in the power of the king and his party.

At this time Paris was garrisoned by a force of 4,750 men of the National Guard, 4,400 troops of the line, 1,100 veteran battalions, 1,300 gendarmes or police.

The first sign of resistance came from the press. Four of the principal editors met and issued the following manifesto which was printed in the *National*:

"Legal government is interrupted and the reign of force has commenced. In the situation in which we are placed obedience ceases to be a duty. The citizens first called upon to obey are the writers of journals; they ought to give the first example of resistance to authority which has divested itself of legal character."

On the morning of the 27th the police began to seize types and break presses. They were resisted in many places. At the offices of the *Temps* and *National* the police were refused admission. Whilst they were attempting to break in the printing of papers went on and copies of the paper were thrown out of the windows as fast as they were printed. Bought up by the crowd these papers were quickly carried all over Paris.

Locksmiths and blacksmiths were brought to break open the door, but they refused to act, and eventually this had to be done by a convict blacksmith brought from the prison. When the police entered they destroyed all the machines.

The example of resistance fired the whole city, and great mobs marched everywhere. The residence of the Premier was protected by a battalion of guards and two pieces of cannon, and a division of lancers patrolled the immediate neighbourhood. Three battalions were in front of the Palais Royal, the Place Louis XI was held by two battalions of guards and two guns, and in the Place Vendôme were detachments of regiments of the line. Thus all the great squares were held by the military.

The police attempted to clear the streets and failed, and soldiers were ordered to assist. As they pushed the people back in the Rue St. Honorè the first shot was fired from a house in that thoroughfare. It came from a shot gun and wounded some of the soldiers.

The troops fired at the house, and the crowd fell away. As the soldiers pursued they were stopped by a barricade made out of an overturned omnibus beside which had been piled all kinds of furniture and other obstructions. But as those behind this barricade were only armed with stones the soldiery after firing several volleys easily stormed it.

In other places fighting took place, in one a police guardhouse was stormed, and the arms carried off.

Next day, the 28th, the people attacked all the gunmakers' shops and took possession of the arms and equipment. Barricades were erected all over the city, and police guardhouses attacked and taken. The working class from the Faubourgs organised and marched upon the City Hall, or Hotel de Ville, and arms were distributed from various centres.

The military planned to enter the barricaded districts in four columns at four tactical points. The first column entering by the richer parts of the city met with little opposition.

The second column entered by Porte St. Martin, and was met by sharp firing. After firing two rounds from the artillery, and a number from the muskets of the infantry it crushed the opposition at this point, but as it advanced into the centre of the city the insurgents built barricades behind it, and the further it advanced the more barricades they built in its rear. It reached its objective, the great square of the Place de la Bastille, but when it attempted to return was stopped by the aforementioned barricades, and fired upon from all the intersecting streets. The commanding officer, after several fruitless attempts to return by the route marked out for him, at last fearing that he would lose his artillery, broke out in another direction, leaving the ground he had occupied in the hands of the insurgents, and reaching a point entirely out of touch with the General in command. This column had passed through the insurgents, but it had left them just as it had found them, except, as one writer remarks, "that they had been taught to meet the royal troops without fear, and to know the value of the method of fighting they had adopted."

The third column reached a huge market place, the Marché des Innocens, but at this point was assailed with a hot fire from the roofs and windows, accompanied by showers of slates, stones, bottles, and scrap iron. One battalion was ordered to march along the Porte St. Denis, clear it, and march back again. In doing so it encountered a barricade in front of a large building, the Cour Batave. Here the insurgents had got inside the courtyard, and fired from behind the iron railing around this building, lying on the ground behind the stones into which the railings were fixed, and keeping up a murderous fire on the troops as the latter body laboured to destroy the barricade. This battalion also was unable to fight its way back, as barricades had been erected behind it as it passed. Its companion battalion at the market place awaiting its return found itself hemmed in, with barricades rising rapidly in all the surrounding streets, and a merciless fire pouring in on it at every opportunity. At last in despair it was resolved to send out a messenger for help.

An aide-de-camp shaved off his moustache, got into the clothes of a market porter, and succeeded in getting through the insurgent lines with a message to the commander-in-chief of the Paris district. Help was sent in the shape of another battalion which had to fight its way in. At the market place the forces united, and fought their way out with great loss.

The fourth column was directed to reach the City Hall, the Hotel de Ville. It was divided in two. One part marching across a suspension bridge was attacked by the insurgents, but bringing up artillery and receiving reinforcements of another battalion fought its way through, and reached its objective – the Hotel de Ville and adjacent Place de Grève. The insurgents barricaded all the surrounding side streets, and kept up a fire from all the corners and windows. One writer says:

"The guns attached to the guards were found to occasion only embarrassment."

Eventually finding the place untenable they fought their way out, attacked all the way by the people who closed in like a sea as the troops passed.

The end of the day's fighting found the people everywhere in possession. Next day fresh troops arrived from the country outside Paris, but great preparations had been made to receive them. Streets had been torn up, and pavements converted into barricades. Great mounds were placed across the streets, barrels filled with earth and stones; planks, poles, and every conceivable kind of obstacle utilised to create barricades. Carts, carriages, hackney coaches, drays, wheelbarrows had been seized and overturned, and trees cut down and used to improvise street fortresses.

Then a peculiar thing took place. The troops refused to advance into the streets, and in turn fortified themselves in their positions. This gave the insurgents opportunity to organise themselves and plan their fight more systematically. When they advanced against the troops, after some fighting the soldiery were driven from their central position – the Louvre, some of the regiments of the line surrendered, and the city was abandoned by the troops.

The Revolution had won.

Remarks

Like the fighting in Brussels narrated in a previous issue the chief characteristic of the Paris fighting in this Revolution was the elusive nature of the insurgent forces. The conquest of a street by the royal troops was not worth the blood it had cost them, for as soon as they passed onwards fresh barricades were erected in their rear on the very ground they had just conquered. No sooner did they fight their way in than it became necessary for them to fight their way out again. They only commanded the ground they occupied, and the surrounding barricades shutting off their supplies and communications made the position untenable. To have successfully resisted the revolution would have required an army sufficient to occupy in force every inch of ground they passed, with another force massed at some tactical point strong enough to assist any part of the long drawn out line at any point where it might have been attacked.

Lexington

The first blood shed in actual fighting in the American Revolution was shed at Lexington, Massachusetts on April 19th, 1775. Then was fired "the shot heard round the world", the shot whose echoes were as bugle calls summoning a nation to life.

The dispute between the British Parliament and the American colonists had been gradually drawing to a head: The town of Boston which had led in the agitation against the oppressive action of the British Government was filled with British troops intended to intimidate the Americans, and these latter had begun to collect arms and ammunition and to store them in various places inland in order to be prepared for any eventuality. At that time the odds seemed so great against the Americans that few of them dreamt of asserting the independence of the thirteen colonies.

The colonies were but thinly populated, means of communication were very imperfect, roads were bad, and no real bond of cohesion existed. The British had a great fleet dominating the Atlantic sea coast, and able to hurl an army at any point where resistance might be contemplated and crush it before it could attain to any strength. The bad roads, sparse population and almost trackless wilds on the other hand made it difficult to unite the Americans sufficiently to oppose the British expedition. Also large sections of the population were ultra loyal, and resolved to stand by England against their fellow colonists. Owing to all these factors there was still some hope of a peaceful issue of the dispute until the occurrence we are about to describe swept the talkers and doubters aside, and placed the issue in the hands of armed forces.

On the night of the 18th and morning of the 19th April the British General Gage in command at Boston sent an expedition into the interior for the purpose of destroying certain stores of arms and ammunition the Americans were gathering at the village of Lexington. This expedition embarked secretly on boats at Boston, and were rowed up the Charles River to a landing place known as Phipp's Farm. From there they pushed hurriedly on to the town of Concord, which they reached about five in the morning. Every effort had been made to keep their movements secret, mounted officers and scouts scoured the country and arrested every inhabitant they found upon the roads to keep them from giving the alarm. But the alarm had been given; one mounted citizen, Paul Revere, having ridden ahead of them and spread the alarm far and wide. Bells were rung, fires lighted and guns fired in order to rouse the sleeping inhabitants by those who received the word as Revere passed on his way.

On reaching Lexington the soldiers found the American militia drawn up to receive them. The Officer in command ordered the Americans to disperse; these latter refused, and the soldiers fired, killing eight men and wounding several others.

The Americans fled and the soldiers then proceeded to Concord, sending six companies ahead to seize two bridges beyond the town that they might cut off the retreat of any armed forces opposing them. The American militia at this point retired and the main body of soldiers took possession of the place. At once they set about destroying all stores; three guns, a quantity of carriages, and a large accumulation of powder and ball were thrown into the river. A number of barrels of flour were also thrown in the same place and spoilt. All this time the bells had been summoning the people, bonfires were on every hill, and couriers were speeding along every road with the news that the soldiers were on the warpath. The farmers and townspeople were hurrying from all quarters to the scene.

Upon completion of their work of destruction the army commenced to retire. But here the first real fighting of the day began.

As the infantry prepared to leave the town they tried to destroy the bridges behind them. A company of militia strove to cross in order to save some of their stores, but the soldiers fired, killing two men. The Americans returned the fire, and the regulars were forced to retreat, leaving behind them some killed and wounded, and a lieutenant and a number of soldiers taken prisoners.

As the army retired the whole countryside rose around them. Skirmish followed skirmish, houses, walls, hedges, woods, ditches were lined by riflemen who never ventured into close quarters, but kept up the pursuit, tracking the soldiers as hunters track game. At Lexington the retreating army was reinforced by Lord Percy with 16 companies of infantry, a detachment of marines, and two cannon.

From Lexington to Boston is sixteen miles and all the way the troops had to fight. The people closed in to firing distance only, crawled along the ground in their rear, lay in wait behind hillocks, trees, and hedges, firing upon the troops, and never exposing themselves.

For the soldiers it was a terrible experience, as their enemy seemed to rise out of the ground. Front and rear and flanks were alike engaged all the time, and every moment required every sense to be on the alert. Eventually the soldiers reached Charleston, and boats took them off to Boston under the shelter of the fleet.

The British admitted the loss of 273 men killed and wounded, and 2 lieutenants and 20 men taken prisoners. Amongst the seriously wounded were Colonel Smith, the commander of the expedition, a lieutenant-colonel and several other officers.

The total American loss was only 60 killed and wounded.

Remarks

The battle of Lexington was a victory for the British, inasmuch as they succeeded in their object, viz., to destroy the stores of ammunition at Lexington. But it was also a victory for the rebels, as they held the ground after the battle, compelled the enemy to retreat, and inflicted more loss upon him in the retreat than they had suffered in the battle. In this respect Lexington was like all the battles of the War of the Revolution. In practically all of those earlier battles the regular soldiers won, but after each of them the American Army gained in strength and discipline. Lexington destroyed the belief in the invincibility of the regular soldiers, gave courage to those who dreaded them because of their perfection in mechanical drill, and gave faith to those doubters who failed to recognise that no nation can be enslaved if its people think death less hateful than bondage.

June 1848

In February, 1848, the monarchy of Louis Phillippe was destroyed by an insurrection in the streets of Paris, supported by risings in various parts of the country. This insurrection, like all previous risings of the same description, owed its success principally to the determined fighting of the working class. But whereas in previous insurrections the working class after doing the fighting were content to let the middle class reap the harvest, it resolved this time to demand certain guarantees for itself.

Education had progressed rapidly, and in addition the relative numbers of the workers were greater than at any other similar crisis. Hhence, after the victory, whilst arms were still in its hands, it demanded that the new government establish in its social constitution some provisions making for social well-being. The government consented reluctantly but with great show of zeal for the cause of labour, and established 'National Workshops', guaranteeing work to all comers.

This proposition was, of course, economically unsound and bound to fail, but it placated the workers for the time. The Republican Government got time to mature its plans against republicanism, and to organise its military force against labour. Thousands of workers were taken on in the workshops, and middle class poets talked enthusiastically and sang ecstatically about the Era of Labour. But all the time the government was quietly drafting its forces into Paris, removing from Paris all the city regiments and replacing them with battalions from remote country districts, perfecting its artillery, and calmly preparing to crush the workers should they persist in their idea that the Republic ought to regard them as its children, not as its slaves. Eventually when all was ready the government began to dismiss men in thousands from the National Workshops, and to form brigades of workers to be removed from Paris ostensibly to work at canal construction in the provinces.

One of these brigades was formed of 14,000 men, almost all of whom were Parisians, and members of various local Labour clubs. In addition to this wholesale removal of workers to unfamiliar provinces, the government on the 22nd June, 1848, summarily dismissed 3,000 more on the pretence that they were not born in Paris, and ordered them to leave the city at once. Money and tickets were supplied to them to pay their lodgings along the road to their birthplaces.

Out of this deportation sprung the Insurrection of June, 1848.

About 400 of the deported workmen returned to the city that evening and paraded the streets, calling upon their comrades to resist the plot of the government to destroy the Labour forces. In the morning the sound of the generale, the popular drum beat to arms, was sounded, and barricades began to be erected in the streets. All the working class districts rapidly rose, and the insurgents fortified their quarters so rapidly and skilfully that it was quite evident that astute minds had been busy amongst them preparing to meet the schemes of the government.

At the Porte St. Denis the fighting began. The barricade here was stormed alter the soldiers had been twice beaten off. At the Porte St. Martin and at several other points similar fights took place, at each of them the soldiery stormed the barricade. But at each of them it was found that after the barricade had become untenable the insurgents were able to fall back behind others that had been prepared for the purpose, and when the troops sought to pursue them they were met by a galling and terrible fire from all the side streets and houses. The insurgents had seized houses which commanded the passage of the streets, but were still so retired that they could not be swept from the front, and had prepared their house in the most scientific manner. The front walls were loopholed, the entrances were barricaded with furniture, boxes, trunks, and obstacles of all kinds, the party walls were cut through so that only one man at a time could pass, and as fast as one house was taken in desperate hand-to-hand fighting they retired through this passage to the next.

Some of the houses were compared to rabbit warrens, full of holes and galleries, and in every corner death was waiting for the soldiers. Windows were blocked with mattresses and sandbags, and marksmen fired from behind them, and women were busy casting bullets, raining slates and stones on the heads of the troops, carrying arms, and tending the wounded.

Before nightfall the troops had been driven back at numerous points, and the roar of artillery was heard all over the city.

Next morning it was found that most of the barricades destroyed during the day had been erected again during the night. To enumerate here the places and districts fortified would be a useless display of names, but sufficient to say that the insurgents had drawn a huge semi-circle around a vast portion of Paris, had erected barricades in a practically continuous line all along their front, had carefully prepared the houses and buildings at tactically strong points, and were now applying to their service everything within their lines that foresight or prudence could suggest.

Two great buildings served as headquarters in the various districts. The headquarters of the North were in the Temple, those of the South in the Pantheon, and in the centre the Hospital of the Hotel Dieu had been seized and held as the strategical bureau of the whole insurrection.

Meanwhile the soldiers in overwhelming numbers were being rushed to Paris from all the provincial centres, and as France was then at peace with all foreign powers the whole force of the army was available. General Cavaignac issued a proclamation that "if at noon the barricades are not removed, mortars and howitzers will be brought by which shells will be thrown, which will explode behind the barricades and in the apartments of the houses occupied by the insurgents."

No one heeded his threat, and on the next day the fighting recommenced. But the shortage of ammunition on the part of the insurgents told heavily against them, and in addition, as the government had all along planned, the soldiers brought to Paris outnumbered the armed men in revolt, as well as being possessed of all the advantage of a secure source of supplies.

The first fighting at the Clos St. Lazare was typical of the whole and therefore the following description from the pen of an eye-witness is worth reproducing. He says:

"The barricades in advance of the harriers were as formidable as regular engineers would have constructed, and were built of paving stones of a hundredweight each, and blocks of building stone cut for building a hospital, and weighing tons. The houses covering them were occupied. The tall houses at the barriers were occupied and the windows removed. The houses on the opposite side of the Boulevard were, moreover, in the possession of the rebels and manned with marksmen. What formed, however, the strength of their position was the perforation of the wall of the city which is twelve or fourteen feet high, at intervals of eight or ten yards for a mile in length, with several hundred loopholes of about six inches in diameter. During all Saturday and Sunday a constant and deadly fire was kept up from these loopholes on troops who could hardly see their opponents.

"The defenders ran from loophole to loophole with the agility of monkeys. They only left the cover of the high wall to seek ammunition, of which they had only a scanty and precarious supply."

Socialism and the Irish Rebellion

It was only when the insurgents' ammunition gave out that the artillery became formidable. Then it was able to pound to ruins the building in which the insurgents were awaiting their attack, and to gradually occupy the district so cleared of its defenders.

By the 25th June all fighting had ceased in Paris. The isolation of that city from all provincial support, combined with the overwhelming number of the soldiery had won the day.

On the 10th of December 1848, Prince Louis Napoleon was elected President of the Republic, and four years afterwards he destroyed it by the aid of the army which the republican government had turned against the workers of Paris in the fighting just chronicled. When Louis Napoleon was destroying the French Republic its middle class supporters called in vain for the support of the brave men they had betrayed in June 1848.

Remarks

The insurrection of June 1848 in Paris was the most stubbornly fought, and the most scientifically conducted, of any of the revolutions or attempts at revolutions in Paris. The lessons are invaluable for all students of warfare who wish to understand the defence and attack of cities, towns, villages, or houses. Whatever changes have come about as a result of the development of firearms and the introduction of smokeless powder have operated principally in increasing the power of the defence. In our next week's issue we propose to sum up the military lessons of all the great uprisings dealt with in these notes up to the present.

Street Fighting – Summary

A complete summary of the lessons to be derived from the military events we have narrated in these chapters during the past few months would involve the writing of a very large volume. Indeed it might truly be urged that the lessons are capable of such infinite expansion that no complete summary is possible.

In the military sense of the term what after all is a street? A street is a defile in a city. A defile is a narrow pass through which troops can only move by narrowing their front, and therefore making themselves a good target for the enemy. A defile is also a difficult place for soldiers to manoeuvre in, especially if the flanks of the defile are held by the enemy.

A mountain pass is a defile the sides of which are constituted by the natural slopes of the mountain sides, as at the Scalp. A bridge over a river is a defile the sides of which are constituted by the river. A street is a defile the sides of which are constituted by the houses in the street.

To traverse a mountain pass with any degree of safety the sides of the mountain must be cleared by flanking parties ahead of the main body; to pass over a bridge the banks of the river on each side must be raked with gun or rifle fire whilst the bridge is being rushed; to take a street properly barricaded and held on both sides by forces in the houses, these houses must be broken into and taken by hand to hand fighting. A street barricade placed in position where artillery cannot operate from a distance is impregnable to frontal attack. To bring artillery within a couple of hundred yards – the length of the average street – would mean the loss of the artillery if confronted by even imperfectly drilled troops armed with rifles.

The Moscow revolution, where only 80 rifles were in the possession of the insurgents, would have ended in the annihilation of the artillery had the number of insurgent rifles been 800.

The insurrection of Paris in June, 1848, reveals how districts of towns, or villages, should be held. The streets were barricaded at tactical points not on the main streets but commanding them. The houses were broken through so that passages were made inside the houses along the whole length of the streets. The party walls were loopholed, as were also the front walls, the windows were blocked by sandbags, boxes filled with stones and dirt, bricks, chests, and other pieces of furniture with all sorts of odds and ends piled up against them.

Behind such defences the insurgents poured fire upon the troops through loopholes left for the purpose.

In the attack upon Paris by the allies fighting against Napoleon a village held in this manner repulsed several assaults of the Prussian allies of England. When these Prussians were relieved by the English these latter did not dare attempt a frontal attack, but instead broke into an end house on one side of the village street, and commenced to take the houses one by one. Thus all the fighting was inside the houses, and muskets played but a small part. On one side of the street they captured all the houses, on the other they failed, and when a truce was declared the English were in possession of one side of the village, and their French enemies of the other.

The truce led to a peace. When peace was finally proclaimed the two sides of the village street were still held by opposing forces.

The defence of a building in a city, town or village is governed by the same rules. Such a building left unconquered is a serious danger even if its supports are all defeated. If it had been flanked by barricades, and these barricades were destroyed, no troops could afford to push on and leave the building in the hands of the enemy. If they did so they would be running the danger of perhaps meeting a check further on, which check would be disastrous if they had left a hostile building manned by an unconquered force in their rear. Therefore, the fortifying of a strong building, as a pivot upon which the defence of a town or village should hinge, forms a principal object of the preparations of any defending force, whether regular army or insurrectionary.

In the Franco-German War of 1870 the chateau, or castle, of Geissberg formed such a position in the French lines on 4 August. The Germans drove in all the supports of the French party occupying this country house, and stormed the outer courts, but were driven back by the fire from the windows and loopholed walls. Four batteries of artillery were brought up to within 900 yards of the house and battered away at its walls, and battalion after battalion was hurled against it. The advance of the whole German army was delayed until this one house was taken. To take it caused a loss of 23 officers and 329 men, yet it had only a garrison of 200.

In the same campaign the village of Bazeilles offered a similar lesson in the tactical strength of a well-defended line of houses. The German Army drove the French off the field and entered the village without a struggle. But it took a whole army corps seven hours to fight its way through to the other end of the village.

A mountainous country has always been held to be difficult for military operations owing to its passes or glens. A city is a huge mass of passes or glens formed by streets and lanes. Every difficulty that exists for the operation of regular troops in mountains is multiplied a hundredfold in a city. And the difficulty of the commissariat which is likely to be insuperable to an irregular or popular force taking to the mountains, is solved for them by the sympathies of the populace when they take to the streets.

The general principle to be deducted from a study of the examples we have been dealing with, is that the defence is of almost overwhelming importance in such warfare as a popular force like the Citizen Army might be called upon to participate in. Not a mere passive defence of a position valueless in itself, but the active defence of a position whose location threatens the supremacy or existence of the enemy. The genius of the commander must find such a position, the skill of his subordinates must prepare and fortify it, the courage of all must defend it. Out of this combination of genius, skill and courage alone can grow the flower of military success.

The Citizen Army and the Irish Volunteers are open for all those who wish to qualify for the exercise of these qualities.

Liberty and Labour

(June 1915)

Decidedly we are getting on! Since this war started we have been progressing at a rate calculated to bewilder the mind of the ordinary man or woman. Especially in the direction of freedom our prowess has been of quite a giddy character.

First, on the grounds that their activities were calculated to hinder the fight which the Allies were making for liberty, the liberties of the Press were curtailed. And as if to emphasise the great truth (?) that militarism must be crushed, the military were sent in to break up the machinery on which the *Irish Worker* was printed.

Then other papers which ventured to doubt the peaceful intentions and liberty-loving enthusiasm of the British Government were squelched in their turn.

Then certain Irishmen were ordered to leave military districts, and under a kind of ticket-of-leave system report their residence elsewhere. We would not presume, being laymen, to doubt the wisdom of the military authorities, but it does seem a little erratic when you suspect a man of knowing too much to remove him out of your jurisdiction. It would seem safer to keep him under your eye.

Next, trial by jury, that great bulwark of British liberty, went by the board, and we have seen men refused the right of such trial, and summarily sentenced to a long term of imprisonment for expressing opinions upon the war.

In all the great wars of England, the war of the American Revolution, the war against the French Revolution, the Crimean War, there were men who stood out against those ventures, and against a nation lashed to madness by the appeals and lies of its leaders. They were but a miserable minority, but history has triumphantly vindicated them.

They suffered from mob fury, and from legal oppression, but none was condemned and sentenced without a trial by jury. The jury may have been, and was in most cases, composed of bitter partisans of the Government, but it was still a jury. The Government of those days did not dare to destroy the civic rights of its subjects on the pretext of military necessity.

Every one of those men, whose names Englishmen to-day delight to honour for their courage in withstanding the tyrants and demagogues of their day, would now be arrested under the Defence of the Realm Act, as other men have been for 'crimes' not a hundredth part as well calculated to 'give aid to the enemy'.

Now we find that a new office has been created, that of Ministry of Munitions, and we are already told that the Minister in charge will have absolute power over the labour and liberties of the subjects whose labour he requires, or thinks he requires, in the factories, workshops, or shipyards of the nation.

All Trade Union regulations are swept away at once, and swept away, be it remembered, with the connivance of the British Trade Union leaders. It does not seem to matter that those Trade Union regulations are the result of generations of experience of what was necessary to safeguard the lives and health of the workers – they are swept away as ruthlessly as if they were but the idlest speculations of Utopian dreamers.

Yes, we are getting on! Our right of a free Press no longer exists, our right of public meeting is a trap and a peril instead of a safeguard, our sanctity of domicile – the privacy of our homes – is continually violated, our Trade Union rights are going where they have not already gone, and all sections of the master class have instructed the leaders of their political parties to support each other against any criticism from the under dogs.

The Coalition Cabinet is the sign and symbol to all who understand that the ruling classes no longer think it necessary to pretend that great principles divide them.

The Liberal lies down with the Conservative, and the Home Ruler with the leader of the Orange hosts. Home Rule is on the Statute Book, but the chief figure in the new Cabinet is the man who organised 50,000 armed men to resist by force its passage from the position of an Act to that of a fact. Could anything be truer than the following remarks, reported in the daily Press, of Father O'Grady, P.P., Chaplain of the Keash (Co. Sligo) Branch of the A.O.H.?

"What, Father O'Grady asked, had they got in return? Could the purpose of the Coalition Government be achieved without inflicting a more deadly wound on three-fourths of Ireland's population than a thousand Zeppelins could inflict? Could any more traitorous indignity be offered by 'the sympathetic Government' to loyal and Nationalist Ireland than the appointment of Sir E. Carson, and the proposed appointment of Mr. Campbell – rebels of years' standing – to positions demanding respect for law and order at least to those who hold them? Twelve months ago Home Rule was a certainty; to-day it is dead."

Carson organised an army to fight the forces of the Crown, but now he is one of the men who will direct the armed forces of the Crown to whatever end he and his may desire. Jonah has swallowed the whale.

We are progressing! O, yes, but whither?

Never was it more necessary for the forces of Labour to be alert, watchful and determined. The classes who control these countries are seemingly determined to utilise every opportunity given them in order to further their class interests, quite regardless of how their schemes may injuriously affect the nation at large.

We have seen the monies promised for the work of tearing down the slums and rebuilding Dublin blown away at the cannon's mouth, along with the sums needed to complete the Land Purchase Schemes; we have seen the war crisis taken advantage of to compel the enforcement upon Ireland of compulsory vaccination without the Conscience Clause that safeguards the English parent; we have seen pliant Labour leaders assisting at the organisation of a Dockers Battalion under military law to do work which civilian Trade Union dockers were willing to do, and we have seen members of that battalion subjected to severe military penalties for trifling delays which in civil life would only cause a frown; we have seen an Englishman arrested for mentioning that the King is of German descent – a fact that said Englishman was taught in the public schools of his country. In short we have seen, and are daily seeing, a continual narrowing of the bounds of freedom, a steady increase of the power of a plutocratic State, a silent, relentless invasion of military power upon the domain of civil law and civil rights.

Against such things it behoves all who value freedom and the possibilities of peaceful progress to organise our forces to make a determined stand. In this matter every man's battle is our battle. Every man or woman who takes up a stand for liberty is our comrade, and their cause should be our cause. No petty personal quarrels should count, no question of the rivalry of organisations, no foolish strivings after exclusive credit for any man or any party. In this battle, the lines of which are now being traced, it will be the duty of every lover of the country and of the race to forget all minor dividing lines and issues, and in contemplating the work before us to seek earnestly after the unity of the progressive forces.

Labour must be the backbone of all the resistance to tyranny. Labour has won a few steps forward and upward, but it has a long and weary climb before it – a climb so long and weary that it cannot afford to lose a single one of the liberties it has already gained.

Already our eyes have been gladdened by the sight of that rally, and from all over Ireland comes the answering shout of joy at the sight. The heart of the nation is good and sound, the courage of the workers not abated one whit.

We are living in perilous times. But we shall not flinch from the struggle.

What is a Scab?

(July 1915)

The question seems rather superfluous. We will be told that everyone knows what a scab is. In Dublin the idea of being called a 'scab' rightly awakens horror in the minds of all honest workers be they men or women. No one likes to be associated with the creature who, when the rights of Labour were in the balance of conflict, when the dignity of Labour was attacked, when the liberties of Labour were in peril, basely abandoned his fellows and 'sold the pass' on his comrades. And yet, as simple as it seems the question involves more than can be answered without a good deal of thought.

What is a scab?

A scab is a worker who in the course of a strike or lock out helps the employer to keep his business going – to dispense with the aid of the men or women he formerly employed. To understand what a scab is we must first understand what constitutes a striker. A strike is an attempt to obtain certain concessions from an employer or group of employers by stopping his business, and thus stopping the flow of profits. If a body of workers are on strike the question of whether they are winning or losing is settled in the long run by their success in stopping their employers' business. If they succeed in stopping that business they win, if they do not succeed they lose. If their Union is able to pay Strike Pay for a year or two years they would still lose if the business can go on without them; nay, if the Union could pay a Strike Pay greater in amount than the weekly wages they had earned they would still lose if the employer's business was going on without them. But if the business cannot go on without them then they win. Hence, and this is the pivot of the whole question, whosoever enables the employer to continue his business without the striking workers is scabbing upon those workers.

Now let us imagine a practical illustration of this case. The labourers in the shops and yards of certain Dublin railway depots are on strike for an increase in their miserable wages. The work of these labourers consists mainly in helping or attending certain skilled tradesmen. If the Companies can get men degraded enough to do it they will bring in men to do the work formerly done by the men on strike. These men will be scabs. But what will be the skilled tradesmen who will accept the help of these scabs, who will instruct them in their duties, and work side by side with them in the effort to enable the Companies to defeat the strikers?

Many of the skilled tradesmen have already signified their attitude. All of them have stood firm in their refusal to do other work than their own. On Saturday, July 3rd, six engine drivers on the Midland and Great Western Railway were asked and agreed to wash out the boilers of their engines. On Sunday the local branch of their Union held a meeting and strongly repudiated their action. On Monday the Company requested the attendance of a deputation to discuss the matter in the office. The deputation attended and stood firm in their refusal. The United Smiths are equally firm, as are the Boilermakers.

But looming in the background is the threat of the Companies to get scabs to help the tradesmen. On the Dublin and South Eastern some few scabs have already been obtained. These scabs first worked a coal boat, and then went into the workshops to attend the skilled men as helpers.

As a result these skilled men are already face to face with the question we are treating in this article.

If a labourer who goes into work on a dispute is a scab, what is the skilled tradesman who accepts him as a helper?

We know how our readers would answer the question, we know how the Transport Union has always acted when another Union had its members on strike from the same employment as our members were engaged in, we know what honour and wisdom would dictate, but –

What will the skilled Trades do? How will they answer the question, "What is a scab?"

For the Citizen Army

(October 1915)

The Irish Citizen Army was founded during the great Dublin Lock-Out of 1913-14, for the purpose of protecting the working class, and of preserving its right of public meeting and free association. The streets of Dublin had been covered by the bodies of helpless men, women, boys and girls brutally batoned by the uniformed bullies of the British Government.

Three men had been killed, and one young Irish girl murdered by a scab, and nothing was done to bring the assassins to justice. So since justice did not exist for us, since the law instead of protecting the rights of the workers was an open enemy, and since the armed forces of the Crown were unreservedly at the disposal of the enemies of labour, it was resolved to create our own army to secure our rights, to protect our members, and to be a guarantee of our own free progress.

The Irish Citizen Army was the first publicly organised armed citizen force south of the Boyne. Its constitution pledged and still pledges its members to work for an Irish Republic, and for the emancipation of labour. It has ever been foremost in all national work, and whilst never neglecting its own special function has always been at the disposal of the forces of Irish nationality for the ends common to all.

Its influence and presence has kept the peace at all labour meetings since its foundation, and the knowledge of its existence and of the spirit of its members has contributed to prevent the employers and the government from proceeding to extremes against the fighting unions. It has in a true and real sense added many shillings per week to the pay of the union members, since it and it alone has prevented the Government doing in Dublin what it has done in Barry, namely, send soldiers in to do dockers' work during a strike. Nationally it has done much more.

When the great betrayal was perpetrated on Ireland, and John Redmond and his followers, aided by all the capitalist press of the country, joined in a conspiracy to rush the young men of Ireland into the ranks of the British Army, the first stirring blow struck against that betrayal was the historic meeting in Stephen's Green on the night of Redmond's Mansion House fiasco.

Who took the field that night in spite of the massed battalions of the British Army, waiting the word in every barrack square in Dublin? It was the Irish Citizen Army sprang into the gap, and by its fearless presence gave new heart and hope to the dismayed and betrayed people of Ireland.

When the first deportation order was issued to the first victim, Captain Robert Monteith, who leaped to arms and invited the people of Dublin to hurl their defiance in the teeth of the Government? Who rallied to the meeting despite torrents of rain, and in face of the open demonstration of armed force by the Dublin garrison? Again it was the Irish Citizen Army.

Who on every occasion on which the enemy has struck his blow at those who stood for freedom has ever hastened to the side of the victims declaring their cause to be its own? THE IRISH CITIZEN ARMY!

Who, when the protest meeting was held in the Phoenix Park under directions of the Volunteer Committee, were the only armed body to attend and declare their adhesion to the cause of their imprisoned brothers in arms? THE IRISH CITIZEN ARMY!

An armed organisation of the Irish working class is a phenomenon in Ireland. Hitherto the workers of Ireland have fought as parts of the armies led by their masters, never as members of an army officered, trained, and inspired by men of their own class. Now, with arms in their hands, they propose to steer their own course, to carve their own future.

Neither Home Rule, nor the lack of Home Rule, will make them lay down their arms.

However it may be for others, for us of the Citizen Army there is but one ideal – an Ireland ruled, and owned, by Irish men and women, sovereign and independent from the centre to the sea, and flying its own flag outward over all the oceans.

We cannot be swerved from our course by honeyed words, lulled into carelessness by freedom to parade and strut in uniforms, nor betrayed by high-sounding phrases.

The Irish Citizen Army will only co-operate in a forward movement. The moment that forward movement ceases it reserves to itself the right to step out of the alignment, and advance by itself if needs be, in an effort to plant the banner of freedom one reach further towards its goal.

Conscription

(November 1915)

We see that the time is now here when it may be very dangerous to talk of opposing conscription in Ireland, and yet that opposition must be organised, and to be organised it must be discussed.

It is to be hoped that whatever discussion takes place now, those taking part in it will recognise that the time has gone past for smooth-sounding generalities, or mere political make-believe. We are now living in an era of ruthless brute force, of blood and iron. Whatever effect public opinion may have in times of peace it has little practical effect in time of war. In times of peace human life weighs heavily in the balance, and the most brutal of our rulers shrink from too readily shedding human blood. But in time of war all such considerations vanish, and the spilling of a torrent of blood in the city streets would cause the ruling class no more compunction than the slaughter of game on their estates.

Indeed that lesson has been all too tardily learned by the people and their leaders. One great source of the strength of the ruling class has ever been their willingness to kill in defence of their power and privileges. Let their power be once attacked either by foreign foes, or domestic revolutionists, and at once we see the rulers prepared to kill, and kill, and kill. The readiness of the ruling class to order killing, the small value the ruling class has ever set upon human life, is in marked contrast to the reluctance of all revolutionists to shed blood.

The French Reign of Terror is spoken of with horror and execration by the people who talk in joyful praise about the mad adventure of the Dardanelles. And yet in any one day of battle at the Dardanelles there were more lives lost than in all the nine months of the Reign of Terror.

Should the day ever come when revolutionary leaders are prepared to sacrifice the lives of those under them as recklessly as the ruling class do in every war, there will not be a throne or despotic government left in the world. Our rulers reign by virtue of their readiness to destroy human life in order to reign; their reign will end on the day their discontented subjects care as little for the destruction of human life as they do.

Hence they who now would oppose conscription must not delude themselves into the belief that they are simply embarking upon a new form of political agitation, with no other risks than attend political agitation in times of peace.

We will not be asked to accept conscription by the British Government unless the British ruling class has made up its mind that only conscription can save the Empire. If it does make up its mind to that measure it will enforce conscription though every river in Ireland ran red with blood.

The people of Ireland have been so long accustomed to temporising, and evading straight issues, that there is great danger that they may fail to recognise the gravity of their action, and attempt to fight conscription as they would attempt a cattle drive, or the making of poteen. That is to say in the spirit of a joke at the expense of the police.

Such an attempt in such a spirit would fare badly against a drastic resolve of the military to 'make an example' of the first conscripts who refused to obey. A round dozen corpses of young Irishmen would strike terror into thousands, but would not affect the appetites of those who daily order to their death thousands of young men in the prime of life and vigour.

Oppose conscription, by all means, but let us not teach those who look to us for leadership that such opposition can be conducted on the lines of dodging the police, or any such high jinks of constitutional agitation. Those who oppose it take their lives in their hands. Let them be made to realise that in advance. A fool, and ten thousand times worse than a fool, is he who would teach them otherwise. Our rulers will 'stop at nothing' to attain their ends. They will continue to rule and rob until confronted by men who will stop at nothing to overthrow them.

Economic Conscription

(December 1915, January 1916)

Of late we have been getting accustomed to this new phrase, economic conscription, or the policy of forcing men into the army by depriving them of the means of earning a livelihood. In Canada it is called hunger-scription. In essence it consists of a recognition of the fact that the working class fight the battles of the rich, that the rich control the jobs or means of existence of the working class, and that therefore if the rich desire to dismiss men eligible for military service they can compel these men to enlist – or starve.

Looking still deeper into the question it is a recognition of the truth that the control of the means of life by private individuals is the root of all tyranny, national, political, militaristic, and that therefore they who control the jobs control the world. Fighting at the front today there are many thousands whose whole soul revolts against what they are doing, but who must nevertheless continue fighting and murdering because they were deprived of a living at home, and compelled to enlist that those dear to them may not starve.

Thus under the forms of political freedom the souls of men are subjected to the cruellest tyranny in the world – recruiting has become a great hunting party which the souls and bodies of men as the game to be hunted and trapped.

Every day sees upon the platform the political representatives of the Irish people, busily engaged in destroying the souls, that they might be successful in hunting and capturing the bodies of Irishmen for sale to the English armies. And every day we feel all around us in the workshop, in the yard, at the docks, in the stables, wherever men are employed, the same economic pressure, the same unyielding relentless force, driving, driving, driving men out from home and home life to fight abroad that the exploiters may rule and rob at home. The downward path to hell is easy once you take the first step.

The first step in the economic conscription of Irishmen was taken when the employers of Dublin locked their workpeople out in 1913 for daring to belong to the Irish Transport and General Workers' Union. Does that statement astonish you? Well, consider it. In 1913 the employers of Dublin used the weapons of starvation to try and compel men and women to act against their conscience. In 1915 the employers of Dublin and Ireland in general are employing the weapon of starvation in order to compel men to act against their conscience. The same weapon, the same power derived from the same source.

At the first anti-conscription meeting in the City Hall of Dublin we heard an employer declaim loudly against the iniquity of compelling men to act against their conscience. And yet in 1913 the same employer had been an active spirit in encouraging his fellow-employers to starve a whole countryside in order to compel men and women to act against their conscience.

The great lock-out in 1913-14 was an apprenticeship in brutality – a hardening of the heart of the Irish employing class – whose full acts we are only reaping to-day in the persistent use of the weapon of hunger to compel men to fight for a power they hate, and to abandon a land that they love.

If here and there we find an occasional employer who fought us in 1913 agreeing with our national policy in 1915 it is not because he has become converted, or is ashamed of the unjust use of his powers, but simply that he does not see in economic conscription the profit he fancied he saw in denying to his labourers the right to organise in their own way in 1913.

Do we find fault with the employer for following his own interests? We do not. But neither are we under any illusion as to his motives. In the same manner we take our stand with our own class, nakedly upon our class interests, but believing that these interests are the highest interests of the race.

We cannot conceive of a free Ireland with a subject working class; we cannot conceive of a subject Ireland with a free working class. But we can conceive of a free Ireland with a working class guaranteed the power of freely and peacefully working out its own salvation.

We do not believe that the existence of the British Empire is compatible with either the freedom or security of the Irish working class. That freedom and that security can only come as a result of complete absence of foreign domination. Freedom to control all its own resources is as essential to a community as to an individual. No individual can develop all his powers if he is even partially under the control of another, even if that other sincerely wishes him well. The powers of the individual can only be developed properly when he has to bear the responsibility of all his own actions, to suffer for his mistakes, and to profit by his achievements.

Man, as man, only arrived at the point at which he is to-day as a result of thousands of years of strivings with nature. In his stumblings forward along the ages he was punished for every mistake. Nature whipped him with cold, with heat, with hunger, with disease, and each whipping helped him to know what to avoid, and what to preserve.

The first great forward step of man was made when he understood the relation between cause and effect – understood that a given action produced and must produce a given result. That no action could possibly be without an effect, that the problem of his life was to find out the causes which produced the effects injurious to him, and having found them out to overcome or make provision against them.

Just as the whippings of nature produced the improvements in the life habits of man, so the whippings naturally following upon social or political errors are the only proper safeguards for the proper development of nationhood.

No nation is worthy of independence until it is independent. No nation is fit to be free until it is free. No man can swim until he has entered the water and failed and been half drowned several times in the attempt to swim.

A free Ireland would make dozens of mistakes, and every mistake would cost it dear, and strengthen it for future efforts. But every time it, by virtue of its own strength, remedied a mistake it would take a long step forward towards security. For security can only come to a nation by a knowledge of some power within itself, some difficulty overcome by a strength which no robber can take away.

What is that of which no robber can deprive us The answer is, experience. Experience in freedom would strengthen us in power to attain security. Security would strengthen us in our progress towards greater freedom.

Ireland is not the Empire, the Empire is not Ireland. Anything in Ireland that depends upon the Empire depends upon that which the fortunes of war may destroy at any moment, depends upon that which the progress of enlightenment must destroy in the near future. The people of India, of Egypt, cannot be forever enslaved.

Anything in Ireland that depends upon the internal resources of Ireland has a basis and foundation which no disaster to the British Empire can destroy, which disasters to the British Empire may conceivably cause to flourish.

The security of the working class of Ireland then has the same roots as the security of the people of Ireland as a whole. The roots are in Ireland, and can only grow and function properly in an atmosphere of national freedom. And the security of the people of Ireland has the same roots as the security of the Irish working class. In the closely linked modern world no nation can be free which can nationally connive at the enslavement of any section of that nation. Had the misguided people of Ireland not stood so callously by when the forces of economic conscription were endeavouring to destroy the Irish Transport and General Workers' Union in 1913, the Irish trade unionists would now be in a better position to fight the economic conscription against Irish nationalists in 1915.

The sympathetic strike with its slogan, 'an injury to one is the concern of all', was then the universal object of hatred. It is now recognised that only the sympathetic strike could be powerful enough to save the victims of economic conscription from being forced into the army.

Out of that experience is growing that feeling of identity of interests between the forces of real nationalism and labour which we have long worked and hoped for in Ireland. Labour recognises daily more clearly that its real well-being is linked and bound up with the hope of growth of Irish resources within Ireland, and nationalists realise that the real progress of a nation towards freedom must be measured by the progress of its most subject class.

We want and must have economic conscription in Ireland for Ireland. Not the conscription of men by hunger to compel them to fight for the power that denies them the right to govern their own country, but the conscription by an Irish nation of all the resources of the nation – its land, its railways, its canals, its workshops, its docks, its mines, its mountains, its rivers and streams, its factories and machinery, its horses, its cattle, and its men and women, all co-operating together under one common direction that Ireland may live and bear upon her fruitful bosom the greatest number of the freest people she has ever known.

Conscription means the enforced utilising of all the manhood of a country in order to fight its battles. Economic conscription would mean the enforced use of all the economic powers of a country in order to fight its battles. If it is right to take the manhood it is doubly right to take the necessary property in order to strengthen the manhood in its warfare. An army, according to Napoleon, travels on its stomach, and that being so, all the things that are necessary for the stomach ought to be taken by a national government for the purpose of strengthening its army. Free access to the railways are vital to the very existence of a modern army. For that reason the railways ought to be taken possession of by the Government on the same principle and by the same business method as it takes possession of a conscript. The Government does not pay the mother of a conscript for the long and weary years she has spent in rearing the son of which it takes possession. No, it simply pays him a few pence a day, feeds him, clothes him, and sends him out to be shot. If he is shot she gets nothing for the loss of her son, as she gets nothing for all the love and care and anxiety she spent in giving him life and rearing him to manhood.

The same principle, the same business method, ought to apply to the railways. All the railways ought at once to be confiscated and made public property, no compensation being given to the shareholders any more than is to be given to the fathers and mothers of conscripts.

All ships come under the same general law. The Empire cannot live as an Empire without ships; the troops cannot be transported, provisioned and kept supplied with the materials of war without ships, therefore as sons are to be taken from their mothers all necessary vessels ought at once be taken from their owners, without compensation and without apology. No matter how much the ships cost. They did not cost their owners as much as the bearing of sons cost the mothers. Take the ships.

Factories also for the production of clothes for the army. The Government should take them; of course you cannot expect soldiers to fight unless they are properly clothed, and you cannot clothe them unless you have the factories to make the clothing. So factories are as important as soldiers. Government is going to take the soldiers from their homes, therefore let it take the factories from the manufacturers. Let it be conscription all round.

There is a grave danger of a famine in this country as the food is limited in quantity owing to the export of so much food to feed the armies abroad. At the same time there is an enormous quantity of splendid land lying idle in demesnes and private estates of the nobility and gentry. This land produces no crops, feeds nobody, and serves no useful purpose whatever. By the same law of necessity upon which the Government stands when it proposes conscription of men it ought also to immediately confiscate all this idle land, and put labourers upon it to grow crops to feed the multitude now in danger of starvation during the coming year.

Will the Government do these things? Will it take the land, will it take the factories, will it take the ships, will it take the railways – as it proposes to take the manhood? It will not. Should it need those things as it does and will, it will hire them at an exorbitant rate of interest, paying their owners as much for the use of them that those owners will pray for the war to continue for ever and ever, amen.

But the human bodies, earthly tenements of human souls, it will take as ruthlessly and hold as cheaply as possible. For that is the way of governments. Flesh and blood are ever the cheapest things in their eyes.

While we are establishing the Irish Republic we shall need to reverse that process of valuing things. We must imitate those who have so long been our masters, but with a difference.

We must also conscript. We shall not need to conscript our soldiers – enough have already volunteered to carry on the job, and tens of thousands more but await the word. But we shall need to conscript the material; and as the propertied classes have so shamelessly sold themselves to the enemy, the economic conscription of their property will cause few qualms to whomsoever shall administer the Irish Government in the first days of freedom.

All the material of distribution – the railways, the canals, and all their equipment will at once become the national property of the Irish state. All the land stolen from the Irish people in the past, and not since restored in some manner to the actual tillers of the soil, ought at once to be confiscated and made the property of the Irish state. Taken in hand energetically and cultivated under scientific methods such land would go far to make this country independent of the ocean-borne commerce of Great Britain. All factories and workshops owned by people who do not yield allegiance to the Irish Government immediately upon its proclamation should at once be confiscated, and their productive powers applied to the service of the community loyal to Ireland, and to the army in its service.

The conscription of the natural powers of the land and the conscription of the mechanical forces having been accomplished, the question of the conscription of the men to defend their new-won property and national rights may follow should it be necessary. But as the Irish state will then be in a position to guarantee economic security and individual freedom to its citizens there will be no lack of recruits to take up arms to safeguard that national independence which they will see to be necessary for the perpetuation of both.

England calls upon its citizens to surrender their manhood to fight for an Empire that cares nothing for their rights as toilers. Ireland should commence by guaranteeing the rights of its workers to life and liberty, and having guaranteed those rights should then call upon her manhood to protect them with arms in their hands.

Whosoever in future speaks for Ireland, calls Irishmen to arms, should remember that the first duty of Irishmen is to reconquer their country – to take it back from those whose sole right to its ownership is based upon conquest.

If the arms of the Irish Volunteers and Irish Citizen Army is the military weapon of, the economic conscription of its land and wealth is the material basis for, that reconquest.

The Call To Arms

(April 1916)

On Friday, March 24th, 1916, Dublin was the startled witness of a sudden mobilisation of the Irish Citizen Army in the middle of a working day – a mobilisation in response to a call coming with the most dramatic unexpectedness. Never was the call so sudden, never was the response swifter or more reassuring in its promise for the future.

For some occult and inexplicable reason the British Government decided upon the instant suppression of a nationalist journal, *The Gael*. The journal in question was the latest recruit to the ranks of true Irish journalism, and circulated mostly in the south and midland counties, but as far as we are aware had not in any sense exceeded the limits of candid and outspoken criticism of those who govern Ireland, and those who support them. It was not jingo, it was Irish, but quietly and thoroughly educational rather than aggressive.

But swift upon the decision of the Government a body of military and police raided the premises of the printers in Liffey Street, seized all the type forms, dismantled the machinery, and carried all the vital parts off to Dublin Castle along with all books and papers connected or believed to be connected with the journal. No explanation was given other than a notification that action was taken by virtue of a warrant from General Friend.

Simultaneously with this raid the police all over the city entered the shops of newsagents, and totally without warrant or legal sanction proceeded to search their premises and confiscate all copies of *The Gael* they could find. Right here in their illegal and bullying proceedings they encountered their first reverse.

A number of the Dublin Metropolitan Police entered the shop of the Workers' Co-Operative Society at 31, Eden Quay, and demanded all copies of *The Gael*. The little girl in charge was not at all daunted by the bullying of the uniformed daylight burglars and coolly answered that she had no authority to give up the property placed in her charge. Then the policemen proceeded to rummage around among the papers. Meanwhile word of the raid had been sent to Mr. James Connolly, who is also Manager of the Workers' Co-Operative Society, and he arrived on the scene just as one of the police got in behind the counter. Inquiring if the police had any warrant they answered that they had not. On hearing this, Mr. Connolly turning to the policeman behind the counter as he had lifted up a bundle of papers, covered him with an automatic pistol and quietly said:

"Then drop those papers, or I'll drop you."

He dropped the papers. Then he was ordered out from behind the counter, and he cleared. His fellow burglar tried to be insolent and was quickly told that as they had no search warrant they were doing an illegal act, and the first one who ventured to touch a paper would be shot like a dog. After some more parley they slunk away vowing vengeance.

Immediately they had gone the Countess Markievicz arrived with news of the raid upon the printing plant of The Gael, and in the belief that this was a prelude to a further general suppression as in 1914, it was resolved to mobilise the Irish Citizen Army to protect the Workers' Republic and Liberty Hall.

Whilst the mobilisation papers were being signed, there came a fresh invasion of police headed by a sergeant and with reinforcements of the police. This invasion was met in the same manner with a request for the production of the warrant. The sergeant said he could assure Mr. Connolly that a warrant was issued, but was told that the reputation for veracity of the police was not good enough for his word to be taken without the document. As the police saw that the forces of the defenders had been augmented, and the Countess amongst others was lovingly toying with a large automatic whilst a number of rifles were peeping round the corner, the sergeant concluded that we had 'reason' on our side and withdrew.

After they had withdrawn the office staff wondering what article in *The Gael* had caused such an action on the part of the British Government, resolved to look through the paper and see. But lo, and behold, we discovered that the current issue had not yet arrived, none but old copies were on the premises, and consequently we had been fighting the police to keep them from taking from us papers that we had not got. We were like Irishmen fighting for freedom in Flanders, and not knowing what it means at home.

Just as we made this discovery we were 'honoured' by a visit from Inspector Bannon and a largely augmented force of constables, all ready for business. To our civil inquiry for his authority the Inspector produced the document in question and proceeded to read it for our benefit, whilst both parties stood lovingly eyeing each other, with their fingers upon the triggers of their weapons. The warrant produced by the Inspector was the original warrant for the seizure of *The Gael*, and its concluding paragraph authorised the police and military to enter all newsagents' shops, and seize all copies of the paper they could discover.

As we had just discovered that we had none of the paper in the shop we informed the Inspector in our politest manner that he could search the shop for it as he had brought the warrant, but would not be allowed to search Liberty Hall, 'warrant or no warrant.' To which the Inspector answered that he would not dream of entering Liberty Hall. We believe him, but they were not always as considerate. No search at all was made, beyond a mere formal turning over of the papers on the counter.

Meanwhile the messengers with the call to arms had been speeding all over the city, and everywhere the boys responded in the most loyal manner. In the machine shops of the railways in factories, in the dockyard, along the docks, in the holds of coal boats, in stables, on carts, lorries and yokes of every description, in buildings in process of erection, the call reached the men, and on the instant tools were dropped, work abandoned, coats hastily snatched up, and within five minutes of receiving the summons the men were on their way despite the threats, promises, or supplication of foremen, bosses, superintendents or owners. Staid middle-class men in the streets, aristocratic old ladies out shopping, well-fed Government officials returning from lunch were transfixed with horror when they beheld the spectacle of working men with grimy faces and dirty working clothes rushing excitedly through the streets with rifle in hand and bandolier across shoulders, on the way to Liberty Hall. Visions of guillotines in College Green, and battues of loyal sweaters fleeted across their visions, and Dublin Castle and the Viceregal Lodge were immediately attacked by batteries of telephone calls imploring the British authorities for news.

In an hour from the first issue of the summons Liberty Hall was garrisoned by a hundred and fifty determined armed men, and more were trooping in every few minutes. It was splendid to see the enthusiasm of the men, and when in the course of the evening all the Women's Ambulance Corps trooped in closely followed by the Boy Scouts, excitement and longing for the battle was running high in all our veins. The Irish Volunteers also were on the alert and stood, we are informed, under arms until after two a.m. on Sunday morning. Since then Liberty Hall has been guarded day and night.

All through Saturday the wildest rumours were current but at Liberty Hall everything was quiet. The men were on the job, and every man was confident of his neighbour as well as himself.

It is understood that every military preparation was made for an attack upon Liberty Hall, but the preparations were countermanded at the last moment. This is confirmed by a writer in the Belfast *Northern Whig* of Tuesday, March 28th.

The Royal Irish Constabulary in Portobello Barracks professed to be anxious to attack us, but the soldiers, being soldiers and not professional spies and bullies like the R.I.C. did not express any desire to make war upon their own countrymen.

The British Government thought to make a coup that would demoralise the national forces, and suppress all their papers, but they reckoned without the splendid discipline of the armed manhood of Ireland.

So endeth the first chapter. Who will write the next?

The Irish Flag

(April 1916)

The Council of the Irish Citizen Army has resolved, after grave and earnest deliberation, to hoist the green flag of Ireland over Liberty Hall, as over a fortress held for Ireland by the arms of Irishmen.

This is a momentous decision in the most serious crisis Ireland has witnessed in our day and generation. It will, we are sure, send a thrill through the hearts of every true Irish man and woman, and send the red blood coursing fiercely along the veins of every lover of the race.

It means that in the midst of and despite the treasons and backslidings of leaders and guides, in the midst of and despite all the weaknesses, corruption and moral cowardice of a section of the people, in the midst of and despite all this there still remains in Ireland a spot where a body of true men and women are ready to hoist, gather round, and to defend the flag made sacred by all the sufferings of all the martyrs of the past.

Since this unholy war first started we have seen every symbol of Irish freedom desecrated to the purposes of the enemy, we have witnessed the prostitution of every holy Irish tradition. That the young men of Ireland might be seduced into the service of the nation that denies every national power to their country, we have seen appeals made to our love of freedom, to our religious instincts, to our sympathy for the oppressed, to our kinship with suffering.

The power that for seven hundred years has waged bitter and unrelenting war upon the freedom of Ireland, and that still declares that the rights of Ireland must forever remain subordinate to the interests of the British empire, hypocritically appealed to our young men to enlist under her banner and shed their blood 'in the interests of freedom'.

The power whose reign in Ireland has been one long carnival of corruption and debauchery of civic virtue, and which has rioted in the debasement and degradation of everything Irish men and women hold sacred, appealed to us in the name of religion to fight for her as the champion of christendom.

The power which holds in subjection more of the world's population than any other power on the globe, and holds them in subjection as slaves without any guarantee of freedom or power of self-government, this power that sets Catholic against Protestant, the Hindu against the Mohammedan, the yellow man against the brown, and keeps them quarrelling with each other whilst she robs and murders them all – this power appeals to Ireland to send her sons to fight under England's banner for the cause of the oppressed. The power whose rule in Ireland has made of Ireland a desert, and made the history of our race read like the records of a shambles, as she plans for the annihilation of another race appeals to our manhood to fight for her because of our sympathy for the suffering, and of our hatred of oppression.

For generations the shamrock was banned as a national emblem of Ireland, but in her extremity England uses the shamrock as a means for exciting in foolish Irishmen loyalty to England. For centuries the green flag of Ireland was a thing accurst and hated by the English garrison in Ireland, as it is still in their inmost hearts. But in India, in Egypt, in Flanders, in Gallipoli, the green flag is used by our rulers to encourage Irish soldiers of England to give up their lives for the power that denies their country the right of nationhood. Green flags wave over recruiting offices in Ireland and England as a bait to lure on poor fools to dishonourable deaths in England's uniform.

The national press of Ireland, the true national press, uncorrupted and unterrified, has largely succeeded in turning back the tide of demoralization, and opening up the minds of the Irish public to a realization of the truth about the position of their country in the war. The national press of Ireland is a real flag of freedom flying for Ireland despite the enemy, but it is well that also there should fly in Dublin the green flag of this country as a rallying point of our forces and embodiment of all our hopes. Where better could that flag fly than over the unconquered citadel of the Irish working class, Liberty Hall, the fortress of the militant working class of Ireland.

We are out for Ireland for the Irish. But who are the Irish? Not the rack-renting, slum-owning landlord; not the sweating, profit-grinding capitalist; not the sleek and oily lawyer; not the prostitute pressman – the hired liars of the enemy. Not these are the Irish upon whom the future depends. Not these, but the Irish working class, the only secure foundation upon which a free nation can be reared.

The cause of labour is the cause of Ireland, the cause of Ireland is the cause of labour. They cannot be dissevered. Ireland seeks freedom. Labour seeks that an Ireland free should be the sole mistress of her own destiny, supreme owner of all material things within and upon her soil. Labour seeks to make the free Irish nation the guardian of the interests of the people of Ireland, and to secure that end would vest in that free Irish nation all property rights as against the claims of the individual, with the end in view that the individual may be enriched by the nation, and not by the spoiling of his fellows.

Having in view such a high and holy function for the nation to perform, is it not well and fitting that we of the working class should fight for the freedom of the nation from foreign rule, as the first requisite for the free development of the national powers needed for our class? It is so fitting. Therefore on Sunday, 16 April 1916 the green flag of Ireland will be solemnly hoisted over Liberty Hall as the symbol of our faith in freedom, and as a token to all the world that the working class of Dublin stands for the cause of Ireland, and the cause of Ireland is the cause of a separate and distinct nationality.

In these days of doubt, despair, and resurgent hope we fling our banner to the breeze, the flag of our fathers, the symbol of our national redemption, the sunburst shining over an Ireland re-born.

CPSIA information can be obtained
at www.ICGtesting.com
Printed in the USA
LVOW12s2008010617
536600LV00013B/741/P

9 781934 941362